THE COMPLETE GUIDE TO PHOTOSHOP'S MOST POWERFUL FEATURE

LAYERS

W9-BSQ-332

Matt Kloskowski

Co-host of the top-rated video
podcast *Photoshop User TV*

**The Layers
Book Team**

CREATIVE DIRECTOR
Felix Nelson

TECHNICAL EDITORS
**Kim Doty
Cindy Snyder
Jenn Concepcion**

PRODUCTION EDITOR
Kim Gabriel

PRODUCTION MANAGER
Dave Damstra

DESIGNER
Jessica Maldonado

COVER PHOTOS
COURTESY OF
iStockphoto.com

PUBLISHED BY
Peachpit Press

Copyright ©2008 by Kelby Corporate Management, Inc.

FIRST EDITION: February 2008

All rights reserved. No part of this book may be reproduced or transmitted in any form, by any means, electronic or mechanical, including photocopying, recording, or by any information storage and retrieval system, without written permission from the publisher, except for the inclusion of brief quotations in a review.

Composed in Avenir and Army Thin by Kelby Media Group

Trademarks
All terms mentioned in this book that are known to be trademarks or service marks have been appropriately capitalized. Peachpit Press cannot attest to the accuracy of this information. Use of a term in the book should not be regarded as affecting the validity of any trademark or service mark.

Photoshop is a registered trademark of Adobe Systems Incorporated.
Macintosh is a registered trademark of Apple, Inc.
Windows is a registered trademark of Microsoft Corporation.

Warning and Disclaimer
This book is designed to provide information about Photoshop. Every effort has been made to make this book as complete and as accurate as possible, but no warranty of fitness is implied.

The information is provided on an as-is basis. The author and Peachpit Press shall have neither the liability nor responsibility to any person or entity with respect to any loss or damages arising from the information contained in this book or from the use of the discs or programs that may accompany it.

THIS PRODUCT IS NOT ENDORSED OR SPONSORED BY ADOBE SYSTEMS INCORPORATED, PUBLISHER OF PHOTOSHOP.

ISBN 10:   0-321-53416-6
ISBN 13: 978-0-321-53416-3

9 8 7 6 5

Printed and bound in the United States of America

www.kelbytraining.com
www.peachpit.com

To my oldest son, Ryan.
You're a great student, an awesome helper,
and a wonderful big brother. But most of all,
I dedicate this book to you for becoming my buddy.
I love you!

ACKNOWLEDGEMENTS

Of course, there are many people behind the scenes that helped make this book happen. One of my favorite parts of writing a book is that I get to thank them publicly in front of the thousands and thousands of people who read it. So here goes:

To my wife, Diana: No matter what the day brings, you always have a smile on your face when I come home. I could never thank you enough for juggling our lives and being such a great mom to our kids while I wrote this book.

To my oldest son, Ryan (my little golf buddy in training): Your inquisitive personality amazes me and I love the little talks that we have. Plus, the Nintendo Wii battles that we have give me just the break that I always need (even though you always win).

To my youngest son, Justin: I have no doubt that you'll be the class clown one day. No matter what I have on my mind, you always find a way to make me smile.

To my mom and dad for giving me such a great start in life and always encouraging me to go for what I want in life.

To Ed, Kerry, Kristine, and Scott (my brothers and sisters) for supporting me and always giving me someone to look up to.

To the folks that make this book look like the awesome book that you see: Felix Nelson, Jessica Maldonado, and Dave Damstra.

To Nicole Wolfe and Margie Rosenstein for your artistic input on many of the projects in the book, and for just being good friends.

To my three favorite editors in the world: Cindy Snyder, Kim Doty, and Jenn Concepcion. Thanks for making me look so good.

To Paul Wilder, our in-house IT guru, for making sure I have a great computer and the software I need, when I need it.

I'd also like to thank our Web team: Jim Gilbert, Fred Maya, Tommy Maloney, Justin Finley, and Kevin Ridgeway. See, I write only a few books a year. However, I literally create hundreds of videos, tutorials, and podcasts that go up on the Web each year. It's because of these guys that I'm able to do that quickly and easily.

Thanks to Scott Kelby for having become a mentor and just all-around great friend. You'll never know how much that one lunch at Ruby Tuesday's helped me when writing this book. Thanks man!

To Dave Moser, my boss and my buddy. Your militaristic, yet insightful, comments throughout the day help me way more than you know. Thanks for continuing to push me to be better each day.

To Dave Cross, Corey Barker, and Rafael (RC) Concepcion for putting up with me asking them, "Hey guys, what do you think if I…?" questions for a month while writing this book. You guys rock!

To all my friends at Peachpit Press: Ted Waitt, Scott Cowlin, Gary-Paul Prince, and Glenn Bisignani. It's because you guys are so good at what you do that I'm able to continue doing what I love to do.

To you, the readers. Without you, well…there would be no book. Thanks for your constant support in emails, phone calls, and introductions when I'm out on the road teaching. You guys make it all worth it.

Thank you.

— Matt Kloskowski

Matt Kloskowski

Matt Kloskowski is a Photoshop guru whose books, videos, and classes have simplified the way thousands of people work on digital photos and images. Author of seven books on Photoshop and Illustrator, Matt teaches Photoshop and digital photography techniques to thousands of people around the world each year. He co-hosts the top-rated video podcast *Photoshop User TV* as well as hosting two other podcasts, *Adobe Photoshop Lightroom Killer Tips* and *Photoshop CS3 Killer Tips*. He's built a massive library of videos and written articles that appear in DVDs, online training courses, and magazine articles for *Photoshop User* magazine. Matt is an instructor at the world's premier Photoshop event, the Photoshop World Conference & Expo, and works full time in Tampa, Florida, at the National Association of Photoshop Professionals.

CHAPTER 6: ENHANCING PHOTOS WITH LAYERS — 154

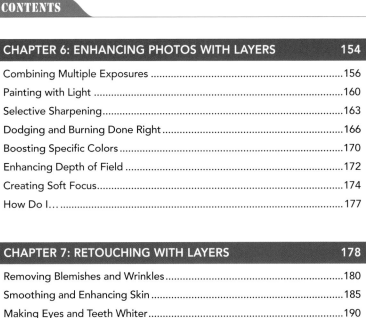

CHAPTER 7: RETOUCHING WITH LAYERS — 178

CHAPTER 8: LAYER STYLES — 202

CHAPTER 9: SMART LAYERS — 226

INTRODUCTION

You know what? I can't stand introductions. I know, it's a bold statement coming from an author, right? It's like some committee got together and said that you've got to have an introduction in your book. Oh, and please make it long. Really long! In fact, make it so long that it will ensure no one reads introductions in your books, or any other books, for that matter. And the vicious cycle begins. That said, I understand the concept of an introduction. It's for the author to introduce you to the content of the book and give you an idea of how best to get the most out of the book you just purchased. I'm going to do that, but I'm going to do it with a very short list (I love lists by the way). Here goes:

1. If you want to follow along with the images used in the book then feel free to download the files at www.kelbytraining.com/books/layers.

2. Feel free to read the book in any order you want. I organized the book into the logical way that I teach layers when I teach it to a live class. I started with the easier stuff and moved on to the more advanced stuff in later chapters. So jump in wherever you want. Hey, it's your book. You bought it, right? You're smart enough to realize that if you jumped right to Chapter 6 and are lost, that the best thing to do may be to backtrack to Chapter 1.

3. Lastly, there's a little bonus in each chapter of the book after all of the tutorials. As an author, it's one of the ways that we wreak havoc on our editors, and we take a small amount of pleasure in that. After all, you can't just make the book about tutorials, right? You've got to throw some tips in, and throw them in at the last minute after all of the chapters are already turned in. My thoughts exactly. So after all the tutorials in each chapter is a page of some common "How Do I…" questions. They're all related to things that you read in the chapter, but I've taken the most common questions and put them into one place so you don't have to poke around the whole chapter to find them.

That's it. That's my introduction. Easy. Simple. Short. Sweet. Getting longer now that I keep adding to it at the end. But still shorter than most. Now, get to it and enjoy the book.

Oh…and thanks for reading the introduction (that no one reads).

— Matt K.

CHAPTER ONE

LAYER BASICS

Here's the deal: this first chapter is named Layer Basics. However, we're going to learn some pretty amazing things about layers and the Layers panel, so even if you think you're somewhat familiar with layers, you'll still want to read through it. That said, if you're pretty familiar with the concept of layers and why they're important, you can skip the first tutorial and jump right to the second tutorial in the chapter—that's where things really start to take off. As for the third tutorial... well, let's just say it gets flat-out crazy. You'll be amazed at all the things that you can do with layers (and all of the little things you never knew about them) after you read that one.

LAYER BASICS

READ THIS IF YOU'RE NOT REALLY SURE WHY YOU WOULD USE LAYERS

Let me preface this tutorial by saying it is only meant for those of you who don't really understand why you would use layers. If you already know why layers are important, then skip this tutorial and go straight to the next one, where we dive right into building things with layers. Okay, so if you're sticking around, then let's talk a little bit about layers and how they're the foundation of everything you do in Adobe Photoshop. Think of it this way: if you were to take a printed photograph, you'd never dream of drawing over it with a black marker and then expect to go back and erase that drawing would you? Well that's exactly what you're doing if you don't use layers in Photoshop and you work on the original image. By the way, as well as making the images used here available on a website (the link is in the introduction), I've also included a video there to help you better understand what you're about to see here, so make sure you stop by and watch it.

STEP 1: IMAGINE DRAWING ON A PHOTO

Picture this: you're holding a printed photo of me. Why? Because who wouldn't love to have a printed photo of me? Seriously, though, it can be any printed photo. The point is, imagine you set that photo down on the desk, grabbed a black marker, and started drawing on it—fake eyeglasses, a mustache, and maybe even a funny beard.

RAFAEL CONCEPCION

STEP 2: TRY TO ERASE WHAT YOU JUST DREW

RAFAEL CONCEPCION

Now what would happen if you tried to erase what you just drew? You'd have to have a marker with an eraser or you'd probably have to grab a damp towel of some sort and start rubbing away at the marker. One of two things would happen: (a) you would start to erase the drawing marks, but you'd probably start to ruin the photo under them as well, or (b) you wouldn't be able to erase anything (if you used a permanent marker) and you'd be stuck with a pretty funny-looking photo.

STEP 3: NOW, THIS TIME WE HAVE A PIECE OF TRANSPARENT PAPER

RAFAEL CONCEPCION

Let's take this example one step further: back up to the point where you have a photo that you want to draw over. This time, though, you also have a piece of transparent paper.

Now, when you place the photo down on the desk and get ready to draw, you place the transparent piece of paper over it. Just like before, imagine taking a permanent marker and drawing over the photo. However, unlike before, you're not drawing directly on the photo itself—instead, you're drawing on the transparent paper. It looks the same, though, right?

RAFAEL CONCEPCION

After you see the final result, you'll probably decide that I look much better without glasses. Once again, try erasing what you just drew with that damp cloth. Now it's a breeze. Or, if you're unhappy with the entire project, then just toss the transparent piece of paper into the garbage and start over again. By using that transparent piece of paper, you've gained a tremendous amount of flexibility.

RAFAEL CONCEPCION

STEP 6: MOVE INTO PHOTOSHOP

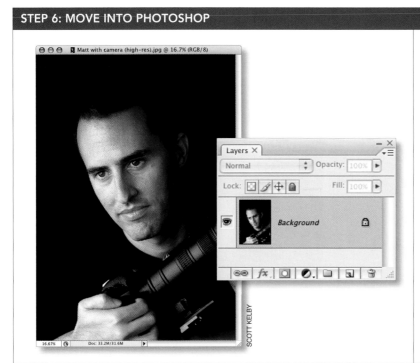

SCOTT KELBY

Okay, enough imagining. I promise we'll actually be using Photoshop for the rest of the book. Go ahead and open a photo in Photoshop by clicking on the File menu and choosing Open (or just press Command-O [PC: Ctrl-O]). Navigate to the photo you want (or just use the photo of me), click on it, and click Open. Now you'll see the photo, but more importantly, notice the Layers panel. If you don't see it, just choose Window>Layers. You should notice that there's only one layer in the Layers panel—it's called Background.

TIP: You can use the keyboard shortcut F7 to hide-and-show the Layers panel, so you don't have to keep going under the Window menu to get to it.

STEP 7: DRAW ON THE BACKGROUND LAYER

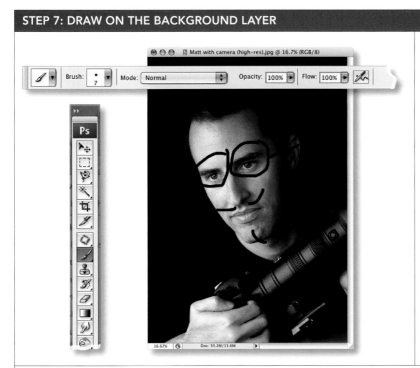

Select the Brush tool from the Toolbox (or just press B) and click on the small down-facing arrow next to the word Brush in the top-left corner of the Options Bar. Select a small, hard-edged brush from the Brush Picker. Press the letter D to set your Foreground color to black and start painting on the photo. Have at it—a funny face, glasses, a mustache, whatever you want!

STEP 8: TRY ERASING WHAT YOU JUST DREW

After you're done painting on the photo, you'll inevitably think it looked much better before the vandalism (sorry, artwork). So, select the Eraser tool (E) from the Toolbox and try to erase those brush strokes away. See what happens? Not only do you erase away the black brush strokes, but the underlying photo is erased as well (you see white here because my Background color is set to white). Not good, but as you can imagine, there's a better way. Go ahead and close this image, but make sure you don't save the changes.

STEP 9: ADD A BLANK LAYER ON TOP OF THE ORIGINAL PHOTO

Let's bring this example back around to the photo with the transparent piece of paper. Remember how well it worked to isolate our drawing on the transparent piece of paper? Well, layers give us the same benefit. Open a new image (or use the same one of me). Click on the Create a New Layer icon at the bottom of the Layers panel (circled in red here). You'll see a new layer named Layer 1 appears on top of the Background layer. This new layer is just like that transparent piece of paper.

STEP 10: USE THE BRUSH TOOL TO PAINT ON THE NEW LAYER

Press B to select the Brush tool again like you did in Step 7. Click once on Layer 1 in the Layers panel to make sure it's selected. Then start painting on it just like before. Everything should look and act exactly the same.

TIP: You've got to click on a layer to select it in the Layers panel. If you don't, then you may be working on the wrong layer. Always look for the layer that is highlighted in color. That is the current or active layer and the one that you'll be editing.

STEP 11: ERASE AWAY BRUSH STROKES THAT YOU DON'T WANT

Finally, to bring this example back around full circle, select the Eraser tool again and erase away any of those brush strokes. You'll see that you can easily erase them without affecting the original photo. That's because you created your changes on a separate, blank layer on top of the photo. You never touched the original photo, just the layer on top of it.

There you have it my friends—the totally basic introduction to layers. Don't forget to stop by the website (mentioned in the introduction) to watch the video and download the images to follow along. Now, roll your sleeves up and get ready—we've got some really cool stuff ahead.

USING MULTIPLE LAYERS

COMBINING LAYERS FROM SEVERAL IMAGES TO BUILD MULTIPLE LAYERS IS WHERE THIS STUFF GETS REALLY COOL

The main idea behind this tutorial is using multiple images and getting used to the way layer stacking works. Working with one image is great, but things get much more useful when you start bringing multiple images into one Photoshop document. There are going to be plenty of times where you want to take a layer from one image and add it into the one you're working on. A great example would be blending multiple photos together to create some type of collage.

STEP 1: OPEN SEVERAL PHOTOS THAT YOU'D LIKE TO COMBINE

First off, open the photos that you'd like to combine into one image. Click on the File menu and choose Open. Then navigate to each photo and click Open. Here, we're going to combine three photos, so I've opened all three and can see them in my workspace.

STEP 2: CREATE A NEW DOCUMENT TO HOLD YOUR NEW IMAGE

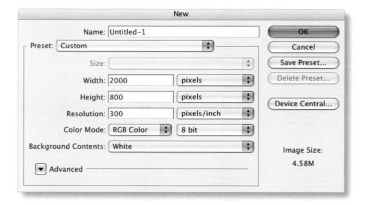

Now let's create a brand new document to hold what we're about to create. Click on the File menu and choose New. I know that I want my new document to be wide because I want to combine all three of these photos next to each other, so I'll make it wider than it is high. Enter 2000 pixels for the Width setting, 800 pixels for the Height setting, and 300 for the Resolution setting. Click OK to create the new blank document.

STEP 3: COPY-AND-PASTE ONE OF THE PHOTOS INTO THE NEW DOCUMENT

We need to get the photos into the new blank document now. There are a couple ways to do this and each have their place. First, let's try the copy-and-paste method: Click on one of the photos to bring it to the front and make it the active document. Click on the Select menu and choose All to select the entire image. Copy this selection by choosing Edit>Copy. Now, click over to the blank document and paste the copied photo into it by choosing Edit>Paste. By the way, we're not going to use the Edit menu for these anymore. The keyboard shortcuts for Copy and Paste are Command-C (PC: Ctrl-C) and Command-V (PC: Ctrl-V), respectively, and they work a lot faster.

STEP 4: NOTICE THE NEW LAYER IN THE BLANK DOCUMENT

Right after you paste the image, you should see a new layer called Layer 1 appear in the Layers panel right above the Background layer. By default, Photoshop automatically creates a new layer whenever you paste something into an image. This is a good thing because it forces us to work on multiple layers. Now select the Move tool from the Toolbox (or just press V), click on the pasted image, and drag it over toward the left side of the new document.

TIP: While dragging with the Move tool, you can press-and-hold the Shift key to keep the layer on the same vertical or horizontal line.

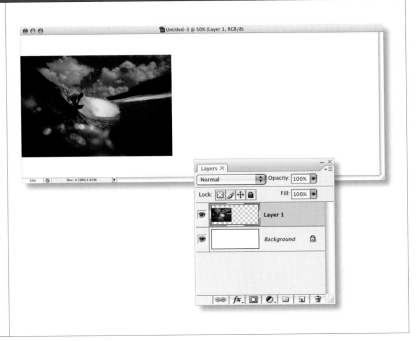

STEP 5: BRING ONE OF THE OTHER PHOTOS INTO THE NEW DOCUMENT

We still need to bring the other two photos into the new document. Before, we used copy-and-paste, but there's another way: you can also click-and-drag images into other documents. Position the new document window and one of the surfer photos so you can see both next to each other. Click once on the surfer photo to make it the active document. Select the Move tool, click on the surfer photo, and drag it over into the new document (that's why you need to be able to see both of them). Once your cursor is over the new document, release the mouse button and your photo will appear as a new layer. Use the Move tool to move it into the middle of the document.

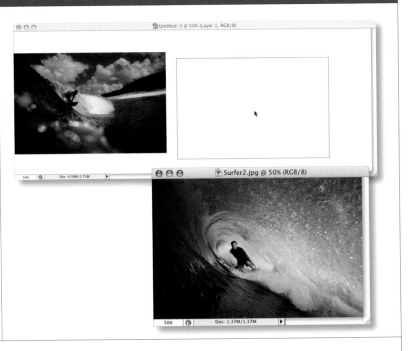

STEP 6: MOVE THE THIRD PHOTO INTO THE NEW DOCUMENT

Another way to move your layers back and forth is directly through the Layers panel. Just like before, set up your workspace so you can see both images onscreen (the third surfer photo and the new document image). This time, click on the Background layer in the Layers panel of the surfer photo and drag it over the new document. As you're clicking-and-dragging, press-and-hold the Shift key. When you release your mouse button, not only will you have created another layer in the image we're building, but you'll also notice that the photo appears directly in the center. That's because you held down the Shift key. Now move this one over to the right side.

STEP 7: REARRANGE THE LAYERS IN YOUR NEW DOCUMENT

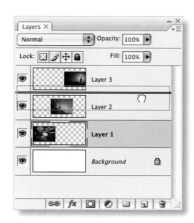

Before you move on, go ahead and close the three photos of the surfers. We don't need them open anymore because we've copied their contents into layers in our new document. Now, notice how part of the surfer image on Layer 1 is being hidden by Layer 2? That's because Layer 2 is on top of Layer 1. Let's swap them by clicking on Layer 1 in the Layers panel and dragging it above Layer 2. Now, wherever they intersect you'll see the contents of Layer 1 instead of Layer 2.

STEP 8: USE THE ERASER TOOL TO BLEND THE PHOTOS

Now we're going to blend these photos into each other. Select the Eraser tool from the Toolbox (or just press E). In the Options Bar, click on the little down-facing arrow next to Brush to open the Brush Picker. Set the Master Diameter to something large like 400 pixels and the Hardness to 50% to create a large, soft-edged brush. Click on Layer 1 in the Layers panel to make it the active layer and start erasing away the right part of the photo—just a few clicks with the Eraser tool should do fine. Notice that wherever you click, you reveal the contents of Layer 2, which is below it in the layer stacking order (so be careful of erasing away too much of Layer 1 and revealing the edge of Layer 2). This makes the two photos appear to blend together.

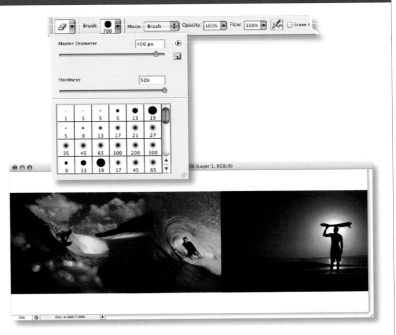

STEP 9: BLEND THE OTHER PHOTO

Do the same thing with Layer 3 (click on it in the Layers panel to make it active and erase away the left part of the photo). Since it's on top of Layer 2, wherever you erase, you'll be revealing the photo below. Again, this blends them together making it look like all three photos were collaged together across the image.

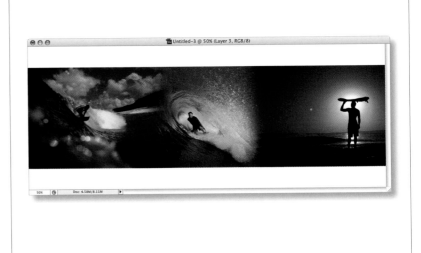

STEP 10: ADD A BLACK BACKGROUND

The blended photos are starting to shape up, but I think they'll look much better on a black background. Create a new layer by clicking on the Create a New Layer icon at the bottom of the Layers panel. This adds a new blank layer (Layer 4). Fill this new layer with black by choosing Edit>Fill. In the Fill dialog, for the Use setting, choose Black and click OK. Now you'll see black over your whole image because the new layer is on top of the others in the layer stack. We'll fix it in a second, though.

STEP 11: MOVE THE BLACK LAYER UNDER THE PHOTOS

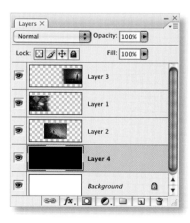

As you can see, the black layer is now hiding everything, so let's fix that. Click-and-drag the black layer (Layer 4) below the photo layers, so it covers the white background but not the photos.

STEP 12: BRING IN A LOGO TO FINISH THINGS UP

Finally, let's bring a logo in. Open the image that has the logo that you want to add. So far, we've been opening JPEG images and dragging them in, but you can just as easily open other types of files too, including Photoshop PSD files. Here, I've got a PSD file that has a logo on its own layer.

STEP 13: MOVE THE LOGO INTO YOUR IMAGE

Before you move the logo into your image, there's one more thing I want you to see: Notice which layer is selected in our new image? It's the black background layer (Layer 4), since that is the one we were just working with. If I move another layer into this image, it'll get placed directly above that active layer. Since that would put the logo below all of the photos, we can save some time by clicking on the layer we want it to appear above. So, click on the top layer in the Layers panel. Now go back and move the logo layer from the other image into this one. It'll appear at the very top of the layer stack, ready to be positioned where you need it.

EVERYTHING ELSE ABOUT LAYERS

THERE'S A TON OF FEATURES, TIPS, AND TRICKS IN THE LAYERS PANEL TO HELP YOU WORK BETTER

If there is one tutorial in this book not to skip, it's this one. Even if you think you know layers pretty well up to this point, this tutorial will show you more. Trust me. See, we're going to build a project. It's a big project, I know. But along the way, we're going to see all the things in the Layers panel that help you work better. We'll look at moving multiple layers at the same time, linking layers, resizing layers, aligning layers, merging and flattening, and even which features in the Layers panel are worth using and which ones actually hold you up. We'll even see how to get around that dreaded locked Background layer so you can actually do something with it. So don't skip this tutorial. By the time you get done with it, you will be a layers pro and the rest of what you read in this book will be a breeze.

STEP 1: OPEN THE IMAGE THAT WILL BE YOUR BACKGROUND

In this tutorial, we're going to create a menu cover. Start by opening the main image that will be the background of the menu (File>Open). Here, I'm using a photo of a dish with a napkin and some silverware.

STEP 2: MAKE YOUR LAYERS PANEL THUMBNAILS LARGER

Before we move on, I've got to share this tip with you. You're going to love me for this one. Ever thought the thumbnails in the Layers panel were too small? Well, you can change them. Every panel has a flyout menu associated with it, and the Layers panel is no different. Click on the little icon with the down-facing arrow and three lines next to it at the top right of the panel (in older versions of Photoshop, it was a right-facing arrow). Choose Palette Options from this flyout menu, select the largest thumbnail option by clicking on its radio button in the dialog, and then click OK. Now sit back and revel in the seemingly inhuman-sized Layers panel thumbnails.

STEP 3: IF YOU HATE THE BACKGROUND LAYER, THEN READ THIS

Notice how the name of the bottom layer in the Layers panel is always Background? By this time in your Photoshop career, you've undoubtedly come to hate that Background layer because you simply can't do certain things to it. You can't move it with the Move tool and you can't change its position in the layer stacking order, either. Well I'm here to tell you that you can change all that. To make the Background layer a regular layer, just double-click on the word Background and click OK in the New Layer dialog. Now it's a regular layer. Sweet, huh?

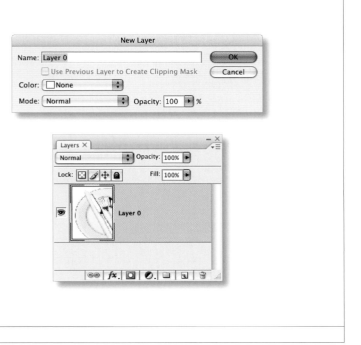

STEP 4: CREATE A NEW LAYER BELOW THE BACKGROUND

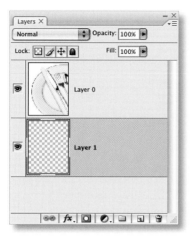

Next, we're going to spice up the plate photo a little by adding a cooler background. Since the photo of the plate isn't the Background layer anymore, we can actually add a layer below it. You could always click on the Create a New Layer icon at the bottom of the panel to create a new layer on top of the plate photo layer and then click-and-drag it beneath it, but there's a shortcut: press-and-hold the Command (PC: Ctrl) key and click on the Create a New Layer icon, and the new layer will automatically be added below the currently selected layer.

STEP 5: FILL THE NEW BLANK LAYER WITH A GREEN COLOR

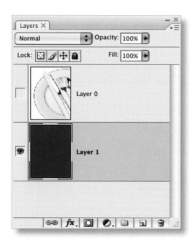

Click on the small Eye icon to the left of the plate photo's layer thumbnail to hide that layer. Now click once on the new blank layer you just added at the bottom and fill that layer with a green color. Just click on the Foreground color swatch at the bottom of the Toolbox, choose the color from the Color Picker, and then press Option-Delete (PC: Alt-Backspace) to fill the layer. I used R: 82, G: 91, B: 45 here.

STEP 6: APPLY THE LIGHTING EFFECTS FILTER TO THE GREEN LAYER

Now, let's apply a fake lighting effect to the green layer to give it some depth. From the Filter menu, choose Render>Lighting Effects. Use the settings shown here (don't forget to click on the color swatches, and set the top one to the same green we used in the last step and the bottom one to a medium gray) and then click OK to apply the filter. (Once you're done setting the sliders on the right, you'll have to click in the preview on the left to move the lighting point and make the lighting area larger, like you see here.) Now you've got a really cool background effect.

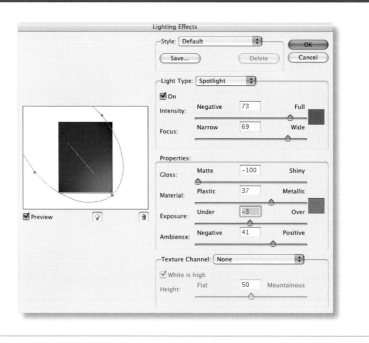

STEP 7: SELECT THE PLATE AND PLACE IT ON ITS OWN LAYER

Click on the empty area where the small Eye icon used to be on the plate layer to show it again and then click on the layer itself to make it active. Now the green layer that we just worked on is hidden. That's because the plate is on top of it and it's got a white background. So let's put the plate (along with the napkin and silverware) on its own layer. Select the Quick Selection tool (W) from the Toolbox and click-and-drag over the white background to select it. Then from the Select menu, choose Inverse to select the plate and not the background. Finally, press Command-J (PC: Ctrl-J) to copy the plate from its current layer and place it on a new one.

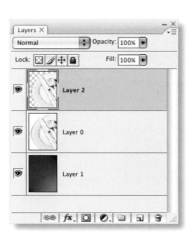

STEP 8: HIDE THE ORIGINAL LAYER AND DROP THE OPACITY OF THE NEW LAYER

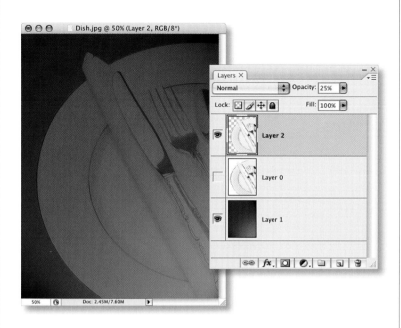

In the previous step, you placed the plate on its own layer. We really don't need the original plate layer anymore (Layer 0), so go ahead and hide it by clicking on the Eye icon to the left of its thumbnail. Then click once on the top plate layer to make it active. Move your cursor over the word Opacity in the top right of the Layers panel. You'll see little arrows appear on either side of the hand cursor. If you click-and-drag your cursor to the left, you'll decrease the Opacity setting, allowing you to see through the plate layer to the green layer below it and fading the plate nicely. Here I set the Opacity setting to 25%. Now our background is done.

STEP 9: OPEN THE REST OF THE PHOTOS THAT WILL GO ON THE MENU

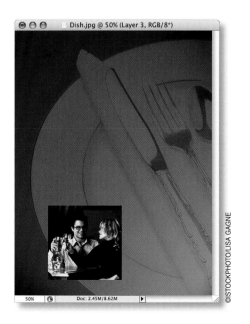

Now open the rest of the photos that you want to include in your image. Here I'll use three food-related photos that will fit well on this menu cover. Let's start with a photo of a couple at a restaurant table. With the Move tool (V) selected, go ahead and click on the couple photo, then drag it into your menu cover image, and place it toward the bottom left of the image. As you can see, it happens to fit right in and is the perfect size for what we're looking for. That's not always the case, though, so read on to the next step.

STEP 10: PASTE A PORTION OF A PHOTO INTO THE MENU IMAGE

Let's move on to the next photo. Just by looking at the size of this image you can tell it's way too big for our menu image, plus, it's not square. So, instead of bringing the entire photo in, let's just take a selection. Grab the Rectangular Marquee tool (M) from the Toolbox. Press-and-hold the Shift key (which keeps your selection proportional) and make a square selection over the area you want. It's okay to select more than you need because we'll fix that in a moment. Now press Command-C (PC: Ctrl-C) to Copy and then Command-V (PC: Ctrl-V) to Paste that selected area into the menu image. You'll see only the selected part of the photo is placed into the menu image and it's on its own layer.

STEP 11: RESIZE THE STEAK PHOTO

We got lucky with the photo of the couple earlier—it was the exact size we wanted. I'll be the first to tell you that it will never happen again. More often than not, you'll have to resize the images you add. In this case, the steak photo is still too big. The best way to resize precisely is to choose Edit>Transform>Scale. Enter the exact Width and Height settings you want up in the Options Bar. In this case, enter 300 px for the Width setting and 300 px for the Height setting. Don't forget to actually type the "px" after 300 (for pixels) or bad things will happen. Press Return (PC: Enter) when you're done.

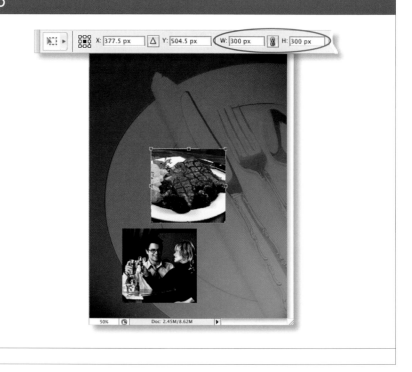

STEP 12: PASTE AND RESIZE THE REMAINING PHOTO

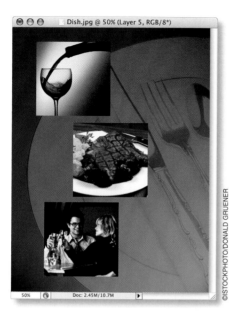

Now we need to bring the third photo into the menu cover image. Make a selection of only the part of the photo where you can see the wine pouring into the glass. Press Command-C (PC: Ctrl-C) to Copy and then Command-V (PC: Ctrl-V) to Paste the selection into the menu cover image. Resize it just like in the previous step, so it's exactly 300x300 pixels in size. Finally, use the Move tool to position it toward the top left of the image.

STEP 13: SELECT ALL THREE PHOTO LAYERS TO ALIGN

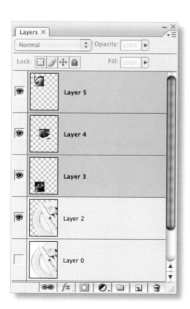

As you can see, the three photos we just added to the menu image are scattered all over. We could try to precisely align each one of them with the Move tool, but it's way too hard to really be exact. Instead, let's use Photoshop's Align Layers options. First, we need to select the layers we want to align in the Layers panel. Click on one of the photo layers in the Layers panel and then Command-click (PC: Ctrl-click) on the other two to select multiple layers. You'll be able to tell that all three are selected because they'll be highlighted with a color (the layers not selected will not be highlighted).

STEP 14: ALIGN THE THREE PHOTO LAYERS TO THE LEFT

Now you need to tell Photoshop where to align the layers. First, choose Select>All (or press Command-A [PC: Ctrl-A]) to select the whole canvas, so Photoshop sees a selection edge around the entire menu cover image. Then, from the Layer menu, choose Align Layers To Selection>Left Edges. This pushes all of the photos up against the left edge of the menu image. It's automatic, so there's no manual effort required on your part.

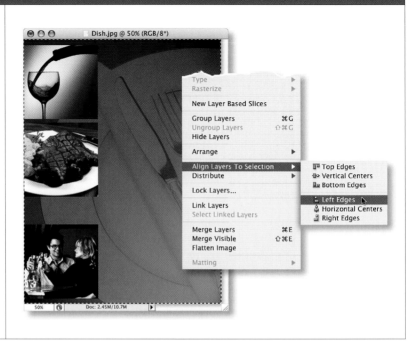

STEP 15: USE THE DISTRIBUTE FUNCTION TO SET THE DISTANCE

Now that the three photos are aligned on the left side, we need to make sure there is an equal amount of distance between each of them. This time, from the Layer menu, choose Distribute>Vertical Centers. This moves the photo of the steak so it's an exact equal distance between the bottom of the wine photo layer and the top of the couple photo layer. Again, no manual effort is required here. Photoshop does all of the math for you. Before you move on, from the Select menu, choose Deselect to get rid of your selection (or just press Command-D [PC: Ctrl-D]).

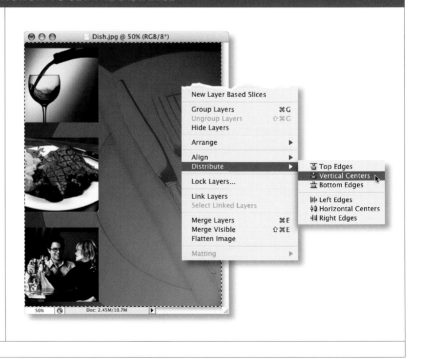

STEP 16: REPOSITION ALL THREE PHOTOS TOGETHER

Remember how you selected all three photo layers back in Step 13? Since then, everything you've been doing has affected all three photo layers at the same time. That's because there is a temporary link between each of these photos, since they're all selected. So, you can manually move all three photos at the same time, too. Try it. Select the Move tool and click-and-drag one of the photos toward the right a little so it's not right up against the left edge of the image. The other two images will follow right along. When you're done, just click on one of the layers in the Layers panel to deselect all three photos and go back to working on only one layer at a time.

STEP 17: RENAME YOUR LAYERS TO HELP KEEP TRACK OF THINGS

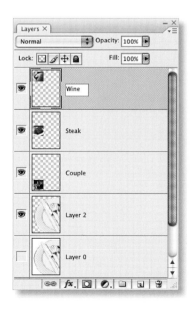

Let's take a break from copying, pasting, and moving for a minute. As your Layers panel starts growing, you should name your layers to keep things organized. Click on the arrow at the top right of the Layers panel and choose Layer Properties from the flyout menu. In the resulting dialog, you'll see a Name field and a Color pop-up menu. But I've got to tell you— that's the lame way to do it. There's an easier way to change the name, and no one really uses color-coded layers, so forget this option even exists. Instead, you can just double-click on the layer name in the Layers panel, the name will highlight, and you can then type a new name (as seen here for the three photo layers).

STEP 18: ADD A STROKE AROUND THE PHOTOS

Now, back to our menu cover. Let's add a white stroke around the photos. Press-and-hold the Command (PC: Ctrl) key and click on the Wine layer's thumbnail in the Layers panel. This puts a selection around whatever is on that layer (cool, huh?). Click on the Create a New Layer icon at the bottom of the panel to create a new layer on top of the Wine layer. From the Edit menu, choose Stroke. Set the Width to 1 px, the Color to white (click on the swatch), and the Location to Inside. Leave the rest of the settings as they are and click OK. Press Command-D (PC: Ctrl-D) to Deselect and you'll see a white stroke around the wine photo. Go ahead and rename this stroke layer something more descriptive, too.

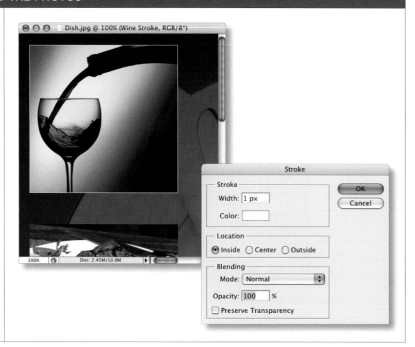

STEP 19: DUPLICATE THE STROKE AND ADD IT TO THE OTHER PHOTOS

Let's duplicate the stroke layer so we can add it around the other two photos. If you click on the arrow at the top right of the Layers panel, you'll see there's a Duplicate Layer option in the panel's flyout menu—there is also a shortcut, though. Remember back in Step 7 when we pressed Command-J (PC: Ctrl-J) to duplicate the plate selection onto a new layer above? Well, if you press this keyboard shortcut while there is no selection, Photoshop duplicates the entire layer. It's kind of a workaround, but it works great and saves a ton of time. Go ahead and press Command-J to duplicate the stroke layer twice and then use the Move tool to move the copied strokes over the other two photos.

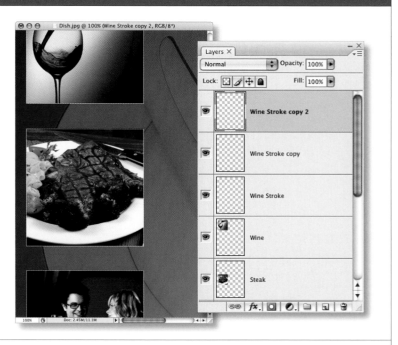

STEP 20: TIDY YOUR LAYERS PANEL UP BY GROUPING

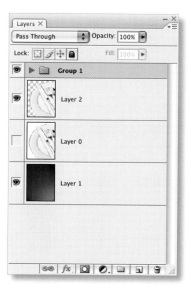

Another housekeeping idea for the Layers panel is to group your layers into folders (a.k.a. Groups). Let's do this for the three photos and their associated stroke layers. Click on the first layer to select it and then Shift-click on the last layer to select them all. From the Layer menu, choose Group Layers. This puts all of those layers into a little folder in the Layers panel. You can click the right-facing arrow at the left of the Group 1 layer to open and close the group so you can see and hide the layers in it. You can also click on the Group 1 layer and move all of the layers in the group at the same time.

STEP 21: ADD A NEW LOGO ARTWORK LAYER

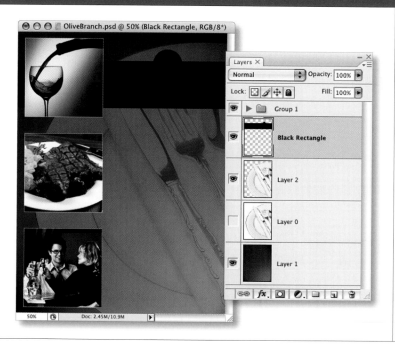

Press-and-hold the Command (PC: Ctrl) key and click on the Create a New Layer icon at the bottom of the Layers panel to add another new layer below the group that we just created. Name this new layer "Black Rectangle." We're going to finish up the menu cover by adding the logo artwork and this new layer is the start. With the Rectangular Marquee tool (M), create a rectangular selection across the image and fill it with black (press the letter D to set your Foreground color to black, then press Option-Delete [PC: Alt-Backspace]). On the same layer, use the Elliptical Marquee tool (Shift-M) to create a small, circular selection at the top of the rectangular selection, and fill it with black, as well. Press Command-D (PC: Ctrl-D) to Deselect.

STEP 22: DROP THE OPACITY SO YOU CAN SEE THE BACKGROUND

The black rectangle is pretty obtrusive and we want it to be more subtle, so drop the opacity of that layer to 40%. We did this earlier in the project with the plate, but there was only a green layer beneath it, so it was hard to see the effect. Here we get something totally different because the black rectangle is on top of a few different layers. We can see through it to the plate and any other layers that are below it.

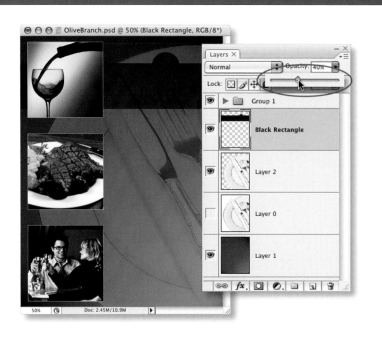

STEP 23: INCLUDE LOGO ARTWORK ON THE MENU COVER

We're almost done. One of the last things we need to do is add the logo and restaurant name. Typically, these types of graphics will be in another image, so go ahead and open the image that has the logo in it. Here, I've got a PSD file that has a few layers in it. One of the layers has the little orange logo in it and another one has the name of the restaurant. Using the Move tool, drag both layers into the menu cover image and position them so they are above the Black Rectangle layer. Then position them neatly on the semi-opaque rectangle as shown here.

STEP 24: LINK THE LOGO, TEXT, AND BLACK RECTANGLE LAYERS TOGETHER

Once you have all of the logo-related layers in place, would you ever really want to move one and not have all of the others follow? Probably not. Well, Photoshop lets you create a link between all of these layers that lasts even after you click on another layer to do something else. To create this link, select the Logo, Text, and Black Rectangle layers. Then click on the Link Layers icon at the bottom of the Layers panel (the left-most icon, circled here in red). This creates a permanent link between these layers so, from now on, you'll only have to select one layer to move and they'll all follow. Now use the Move tool to reposition them toward the bottom.

STEP 25: CLEAN UP BY DELETING UNNECESSARY LAYERS

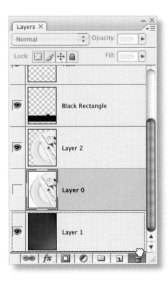

Another task to do often is delete any layers that aren't needed anymore. For example, the original plate layer that we hid earlier (Layer 0) won't be used again, so just click on that layer and drag it to the Trash icon at the bottom of the Layers panel. This is also a great idea to do as you're working because it helps keep file size to a minimum and Photoshop running faster overall. Plus, it just cuts down on clutter in the Layers panel.

STEP 26: MERGE ANY LAYERS THAT DON'T NEED TO STAY EDITABLE

Finally, I'd merge any layers that don't need to stay editable. You see, every layer you have in the Layers panel takes up space in your file and your computer's memory. Plus, too many layers are just plain hard to deal with. Who wants an image with 20, 30, or even more layers in it? So I merge (flatten) layers often when I know I don't need to change something. A great example here would be the small square photos and their stroke layers (which we placed in a group in Step 20). To merge them, select both layers first (as seen here). Then from the Layer menu, choose Merge Layers. This squishes both layers into one. You won't be able to edit the stroke independent of the photo it was around anymore, but you probably don't care at this point. That's it! The über layers project is complete. The only thing left to do is save the image as a PSD file so you can reopen it later and still edit all of the layers if you need to.

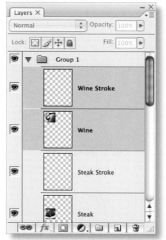

HOW DO I...

? CREATE A NEW LAYER?

Press Command-Shift-N (PC: Ctrl-Shift-N) or click on the Create a New Layer icon at the bottom of the Layers panel.

? CREATE A NEW LAYER WITHOUT SEEING THE NEW LAYER DIALOG?

Press Command-Option-Shift-N (PC: Ctrl-Alt-Shift-N) or click on the Create a New Layer icon at the bottom of the Layers panel.

? RENAME A LAYER?

Double-click on the name of the layer in the Layers panel and type a new name.

? CONVERT A BACKGROUND LAYER TO A REGULAR LAYER?

Double-click on the Background layer in the Layers panel. Then click OK in the New Layer dialog to accept the new name. Or, even better, you can press-and-hold the Option (PC: Alt) key and double-click on the Background layer in the Layers panel, and that bypasses the New Layer dialog.

? DUPLICATE A LAYER?

Press Command-J (PC: Ctrl-J) or click-and-drag the layer onto the Create a New Layer icon at the bottom of the Layers panel.

? MOVE A LAYER UP OR DOWN IN THE LAYER STACK?

There are two ways actually. The first is with the mouse: just click-and-drag a layer up or down in the layer stack. You can also do it with a keyboard shortcut: to move a layer up in the stack, press Command-] (Right Bracket key; PC: Ctrl-]). To move a layer down the layer stack press Command-[(Left Bracket key; PC: Ctrl-[).

? SELECT MULTIPLE LAYERS AT ONCE?

Click on one layer, then press-and-hold the Command (PC: Ctrl) key, and click on any other layers you want to select. If they are contiguous, click on the first layer and then Shift-click on the last layer to select them all.

? GROUP LAYERS INTO A FOLDER?

Select the layers you want to group. Then press Command-G (PC: Ctrl-G).

CHAPTER TWO

BLENDING LAYERS

Blending layers lets you take your images to the next level. There are a lot of ways to blend layers together that go beyond simply changing the opacity. One of those ways is called blend modes. It's like opacity on steroids, and the effects you can get with blend modes are unlike any other effects you'll find in Photoshop. That said, there are a lot of blend modes in Photoshop. My goal in this chapter is to show you only those you really need to know about. Most of the blend modes will probably never get used, so we're just going to concentrate on the ones that you're going to use the most. In fact, turn the page and you'll see the first tutorial is named "The Three Blend Modes You Need Most."

THE THREE BLEND MODES YOU NEED MOST

START HERE FOR A QUICK INTRODUCTION TO BLEND MODES AND WHICH THREE BLEND MODES YOU NEED MOST

I mentioned in the introduction to this chapter that there are a lot of blend modes—25 in the Layers panel, to be exact, plus a few more hidden in some other places in Photoshop. If you had to know what all of them did, you'd probably never get anything done (not to mention you'd be a geek and all of your friends would make fun of you). That's where this tutorial comes in. Forget about the 25 blend modes and concentrate on just the three of them you need most.

STEP 1: OPEN A PHOTO TO EXPERIMENT WITH

Start off by opening a photo to experiment with. It can be a photo of anything at this point. It doesn't matter. We just need an image to work with. (Remember, if you want to follow along using my images, you can download them at the website I listed in the introduction.) We're going to do things a little different in this tutorial. I'm going to go through two examples for each of the three blend modes you'll use the most to help you see what is going on. The first will be a not-so-real-world example of a blend mode and the second will be a real-world use of the same blend mode. I think you'll see that each example helps you understand what's going on with blend modes in its own way.

MATT KLOSKOWSKI

STEP 2: ADD A NEW LAYER AND SELECT THE GRADIENT TOOL

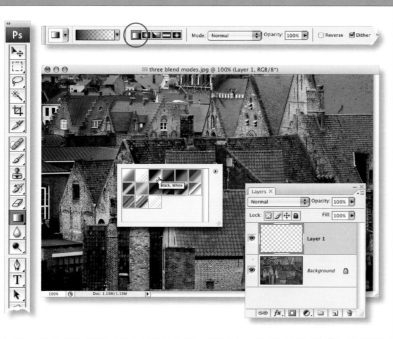

Okay, we need to set up our not-so-real-world example of blend modes. Create a new layer above the Background layer by clicking on the Create a New Layer icon at the bottom of the Layers panel. Then, select the Gradient tool (G) from the Toolbox. Press Return (PC: Enter) to bring up the Gradient Picker. It'll show up wherever your cursor is on the screen. Choose the third gradient from the left in the top row. It's one of the default gradients called Black, White. Press Esc to close the Gradient Picker. Finally, make sure you select Linear Gradient in the Options Bar (it's the first icon to the right of the gradient thumbnail).

STEP 3: APPLY A LINEAR GRADIENT ACROSS THE IMAGE

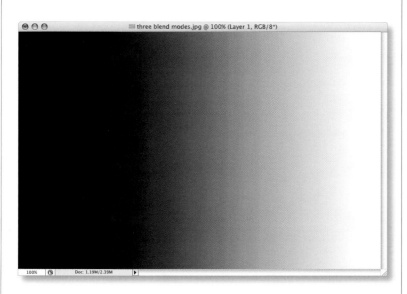

Click once in the Layers panel on the new layer you created in Step 2. Then, with the Gradient tool selected, click-and-drag on your image from the far left across to the far right to put a black-to-white linear gradient on that layer. This is the layer we're going to use to see what's really going on behind the scenes of the three blend modes we'll be looking at.

Let's look at the first really useful blend mode. It's called Multiply. With the gradient layer you just created in Step 3 still selected, click on the blend mode pop-up menu in the top-left corner of the Layers panel, and choose Multiply. So, what just happened? Well, where changing the layer's Opacity setting changes the opacity of *everything* on a layer, changing a layer blend mode changes the opacity of things differently depending on their colors.

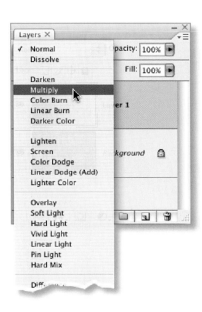

Multiply, for example, always has the effect of darkening, except where things are white. Think of it this way: Multiply multiplies two colors (the top layer times the layer under it). Black times any color will result in black, as you can see from the far left of the image. Gray multiplied with any color results in something darker than the original, as you can see from the middle portion of the image. Finally, white times anything leaves it unchanged and therefore makes any white drop out or become transparent. You can see this on the right side of the image where the gradient used to be all white.

STEP 6: SET UP THE REAL WORLD EXAMPLE FOR MULTIPLY

Now open two images: a photo and a black logo with a white background. Here, I've opened one of the surfer photos we used in Chapter 1, and the logo that we used in that same tutorial. Use the Move tool (V) to click-and-drag the logo image into the same document as the photo so the logo appears on a layer on top of it.

STEP 7: REAL WORLD EXAMPLE OF THE MULTIPLY BLEND MODE

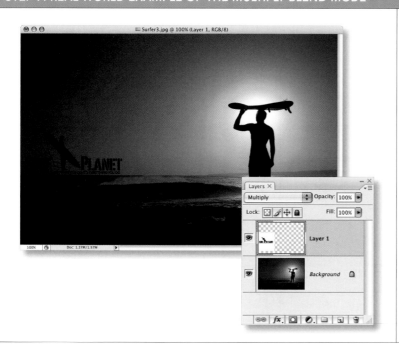

Change the blend mode of the logo layer to Multiply. This is a great example of how blend modes can save you a bunch of time when you're working with simple graphics. Normally you'd think you have to select the white areas and delete them, but it's a lot easier than that. If you recall from the gradient example, the Multiply blend mode drops out all of the white and makes it transparent. Now you're only left with the parts of the logo that were black.

Now let's switch back to the gradient example. This time, change the blend mode of the gradient layer to Screen. You'll notice it looks quite a bit different from Multiply.

Screen is considered the opposite of Multiply. I mentioned earlier that Multiply will always have the effect of making the resulting image darker. Screen, on the other hand, will always have the effect of making things lighter. It's actually the exact opposite of Multiply. Pure white will always look white—it stays the same. Gray will become lighter, depending on how dark the gray was in the first place, as you can see by the gradient. Anything that is totally black becomes transparent and gets dropped from the resulting image.

STEP 10: SET UP THE REAL WORLD EXAMPLE FOR SCREEN

Open two images. Here I have one of those popular ornamental-style backgrounds and a photo of a young woman on a brick background. Click on the photo of the woman, then go under the Image menu and choose Adjustments>Threshold. Set the Threshold Level setting to 99 and click OK. Now, use the Move tool to drag this black-and-white image onto the green ornamental background.

STEP 11: REAL WORLD EXAMPLE OF THE SCREEN BLEND MODE

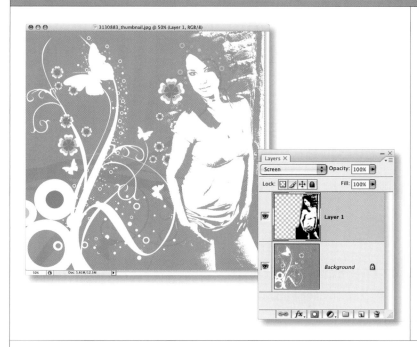

Change the blend mode of the layer with the woman on it to Screen. As you can see, this drops out everything that was black in the image so now you're just left with a white silhouette of the girl. You can even use the Eraser tool (E) to erase away any areas you don't like. It makes a really cool image, especially since that grunge style of design is hot these days.

STEP 12: CHANGE GRADIENT EXAMPLE BLEND MODE TO SOFT LIGHT

The last of the three most important blend modes is Soft Light. Go back to the gradient example and switch the gradient layer's blend mode to Soft Light. As you can see, Soft Light has yet another totally different effect than the previous two.

TIP: Truthfully, the Overlay blend mode ranks right up there as a contender for the third most popular blend mode. It has a similar effect (but slightly stronger) to Soft Light, though, so give it a try.

STEP 13: NOT-SO-REAL-WORLD EXAMPLE OF THE SOFT LIGHT BLEND MODE

If you look where the gradient was black, you'll see the underlying image was darkened. Wherever the gradient was white, the underlying image was lightened. So basically, the darks were made darker and the lights were made lighter. However, anything that was 50% gray became transparent. So any areas in the center of the gradient dropped out just like white and black did for the other two examples (Multiply and Screen). This is all really another way of saying the contrast was increased. That's why Soft Light is known as a contrast-enhancing blend mode.

STEP 14: SET UP THE REAL WORLD EXAMPLE FOR SOFT LIGHT

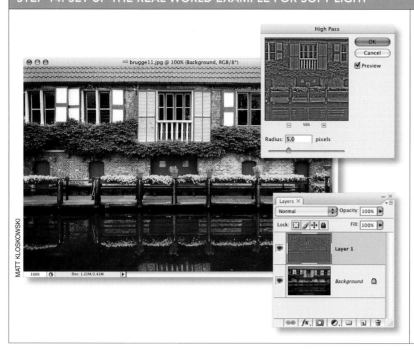

Open a photo with lots of small details in it that can use some sharpening. Duplicate the Background layer by pressing Command-J (PC: Ctrl-J). Go to the Filter menu and choose Other>High Pass. Enter a fairly low setting like 4–5 pixels (just enough so you can start to see some of the details in the gray area of the layer). Click OK when you're done. Notice what the High Pass filter did? It made most of the layer gray (50% gray, actually). However, it took any of the detailed areas and made them lighter or darker depending on their original color.

STEP 15: REAL WORLD EXAMPLE OF THE SOFT LIGHT BLEND MODE

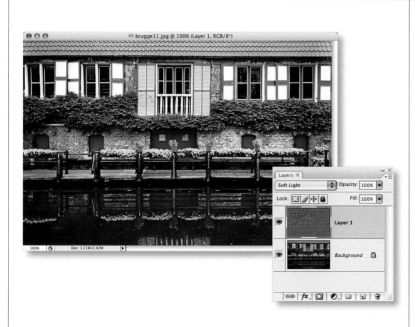

Now change the blend mode of the High Pass layer you just created to Soft Light. Cool, huh? This has the effect of sharpening the photo by adding contrast to the edges (which is what sharpening really does). It's the same as the gradient example: Anything that was dark was made darker. Anything that was lighter in color was made even lighter. Then, just like the gradient, anything that was exactly 50% gray was made transparent and not visible in the final image. We're able to hide the gray and just get the contrast-enhancing effect of the Soft Light blend mode. Oh yeah, the Overlay blend mode often produces a good effect too, so give it a try.

A CLOSER LOOK AT BLEND MODES

LET'S TAKE A CLOSER LOOK AT THE LAYER BLEND MODES AND CREATE A COOL IMAGE, TOO

In the first tutorial of this chapter, you saw the three blend modes that you'll probably use the most. That doesn't mean the other blend modes aren't useful, though. There are lots of things you can do when you combine those three blend modes with some of the others.

STEP 1: OPEN THREE PHOTOS THAT YOU'D LIKE TO BLEND TOGETHER

Open three photos that you'd like to combine. We're not going to create a collage here (we will in Chapter 4, though), so when I say blend I mean it in a different way. We're going to duplicate parts of each layer and use them to blend with the layers below.

STEP 2: CREATE A BLANK DOCUMENT TO HOLD OUR NEW IMAGE

Next, press Command-N (PC: Ctrl-N) to open the New dialog. Set the Width to 600 pixels and the Height to 800 pixels. Then, set the Resolution to 72 ppi, the Color Mode to RGB Color, and the Background Contents to White, and click OK to create the new document.

STEP 3: BRING THE THREE PHOTOS INTO THE NEW IMAGE. RESIZE THEM IF NEEDED

Get the Move tool (V) and click-and-drag each of the three photos into the new document. From bottom to top, I've placed the woman with her arms crossed right above the Background layer. Then, I placed the man with the glasses above her. Finally, I've placed the woman with the dark hair on the top layer. If you're not happy with the way the photos fit, you can choose Edit>Free Transform, or press Command-T (PC: Ctrl-T), to resize them and experiment with a different layout.

STEP 4: LET'S TAKE A LOOK AT THE BLEND MODES BEFORE WE MOVE ON

Before we move on, let's take a quick look at the layer blend mode pop-up menu. Even though it looks intimidating, you can make some sense out of the way it's organized. Each section in the menu can be categorized: The second section from the top (1) lists the blend modes that have a darkening effect. The next section (2) lists blend modes that have a lightening effect. After that (3) are blend modes that enhance contrast. These blend modes will lighten or darken depending on the color, where the other two sections will always darken or always lighten. The next section isn't really all that useful, so we'll skip it. Finally, the bottom section (4) lists blend modes that work with color.

STEP 5: SELECT THE LAYER WITH THE PHOTO OF THE MAN. MAKE A SQUARE SELECTION AND DUPLICATE IT

Let's start creating our blend mode design here by experimenting with the darkening blend modes. First, hide the two layers with the photos of the women on them (by clicking on the Eye icons to the left of the layer thumbnails) just to make things easier to see. Now, click on the layer with the photo of the man on it to select it. Get the Rectangular Marquee tool (M) and make a square selection in the top-right corner. Don't worry if it extends off onto the background. Duplicate that selection by pressing Command-J (PC: Ctrl-J) to put that part of the layer on its own layer.

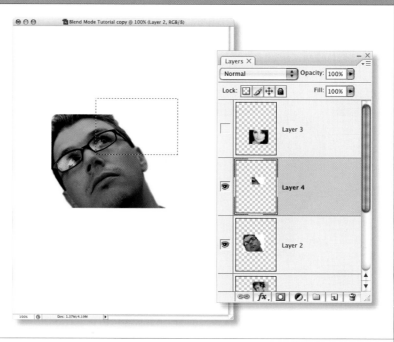

Change the blend mode of the new layer to Color Burn. Notice how it not only gets darker but appears red, too? Any blend mode that has the word "burn" in it will have just that effect. It'll make the image appear burned. This effect is a little too much for this image, so reduce the opacity of that layer to 40% to blend it with the photo below.

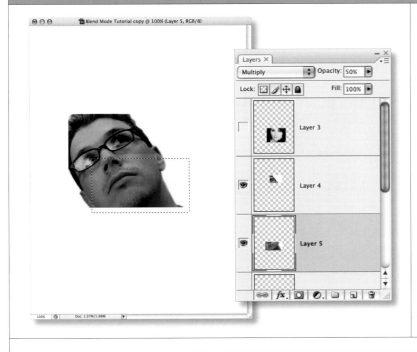

Select the layer with the man on it again. This time, make a selection over the bottom-right area of the photo and press Command-J (PC: Ctrl-J) again to duplicate this selection onto its own layer. Change this blend mode to Multiply to darken it. Then drop the opacity of the layer to around 50% to lessen the effect.

Now Command-click (PC: Ctrl-click) on each of the layers with the man on it to select all three. Press Command-G (PC: Ctrl-G) to group them into a folder to help keep the Layers panel tidy.

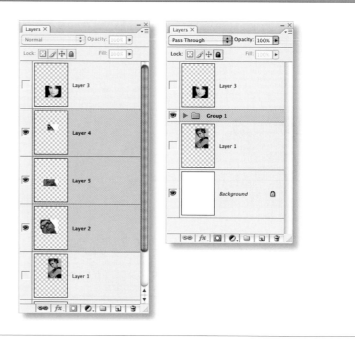

Next, unhide the photo of the woman with the dark hair by clicking in the empty spot to the left of the layer thumbnail where the Eye icon used to be. Her layer should be on top of the group you just created in the Layers panel, so the photo appears above the man with the glasses. Click on that layer to select it. Now we're going to experiment with some of the lightening blend modes.

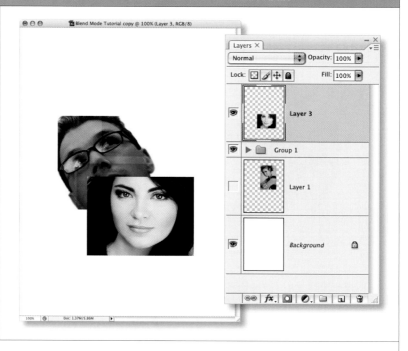

Just like we did in Steps 5–8, duplicate two portions of the layer onto their own layers. Change their blend modes to Color Dodge and Screen, respectively. You've already seen what Screen does. Color Dodge, however, has an extreme brightening effect. In fact, any blend mode that has the word "dodge" in it tends to take any colors that were close to white and really blow them out so they appear much brighter then they originally were. Reduce the effect of the Color Dodge layer by changing the opacity to 75%. Finally, select all three layers and group them together by pressing Command-G (PC: Ctrl-G).

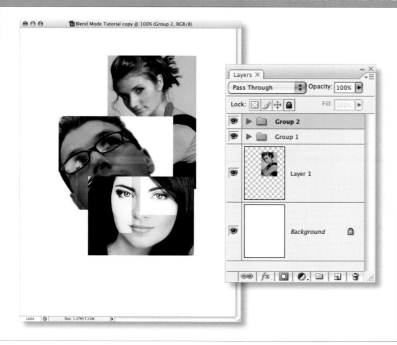

Now let's take a look at the contrast-enhancing blend modes. Go ahead and unhide the photo of the woman with her arms crossed. Make sure this layer is below the two groups we just created in the Layers panel.

STEP 12: REPEAT STEPS 5–8; USE OVERLAY AND HARD LIGHT FOR THE DUPLICATE LAYERS

Once again, follow Steps 5–8 to duplicate two portions of the layer onto their own layers. Change the new layers' blend modes to Overlay and Hard Light. These are both contrast-enhancing blend modes. Overlay does a nice job of enhancing the contrast, while Hard Light gives an even more intense, contrasty effect to the photo. You can even try moving the Hard Light layer to the top of the layer stack and lowering the opacity to 40% to make it interact with the photo of the man and the one of the other woman, too.

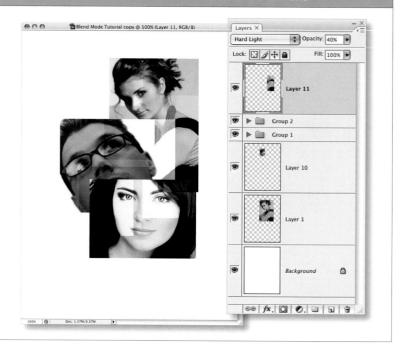

STEP 13: CREATE A RECTANGULAR SHAPE; FILL IT WITH ANY COLOR; CHANGE THE BLEND MODE TO COLOR

Now let's experiment with the color-related blend modes at the bottom of the pop-up menu. First, create a new blank layer, then create a rectangular selection and fill it with a color (Edit>Fill, and choose Color from the Use pop-up menu). Any color will do, really, but if you want to follow what I did here, use R: 168, G: 110, B: 88. Then press Command-D (PC: Ctrl-D) to Deselect. Change the blend mode of the layer to Color. The Color blend mode turns whatever images it appears over the color of the layer on top. However, it has to interact with a color to work, so anywhere it appears over white (in this case, the background) or black it will appear transparent.

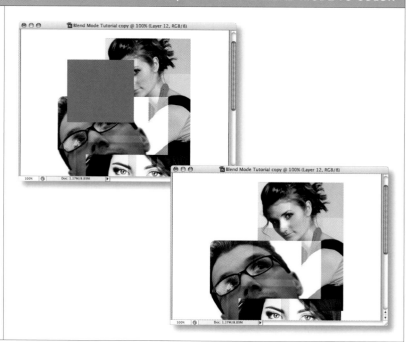

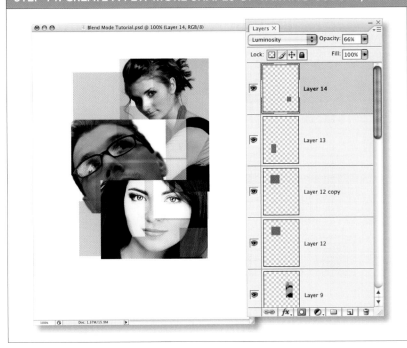

Repeat Step 13 a few more times to create a few more rectangular shapes. I stuck with two colors here: R: 168, G: 110, B: 88 and R: 121, G: 142, B: 145. I dropped the opacity of some layers and tried setting the blend mode of others to Luminosity and Hue. Luminosity generally removes the color from the image and just shows the luminosity values (lightness and darkness). Hence it makes it appear black and white. Hue is an offshoot of the Color blend mode, but interacts with the underlying layer a little differently.

I added a drop shadow to a couple of the layers by clicking on the layer, then clicking on the Add a Layer Style icon at the bottom of the Layers panel, and choosing Drop Shadow. You can tweak the drop shadow when the Layer Style dialog appears or just click OK to keep the default. Here's the final image set inside a movie poster. And the main part of it was all done with just three photos and various blend modes.

LAYER BLEND MODES FOR PHOTOGRAPHERS

HOW A FEW SIMPLE BLEND MODES CAN HELP ENHANCE YOUR PHOTOS

What I really like about blend modes is the fact that they don't change the actual pixels in your image. They just change the way things appear onscreen. As a photographer, this is a big deal because we want to be creative, yet we always want the flexibility to change things as a photo evolves. Blend modes are a great way to get the best of both of those worlds when it comes to enhancing your photos. In this tutorial, we're going to cover a few common problems with digital photos and how blend modes can help fix them.

STEP 1: PROBLEM: DARK OR UNDEREXPOSED PHOTOS

One of the first ways you'll see blend modes can help with photos is when you have a dark or underexposed photo. Go ahead and open a photo that is too dark. Here's a shot taken in Maui at sunset, and it appears a bit too dark.

STEP 2: DUPLICATE THE BACKGROUND LAYER AND CHANGE THE BLEND MODE TO SCREEN TO LIGHTEN IT

Press Command-J (PC: Ctrl-J) to duplicate the Background layer so there are two copies in the Layers panel. Then, change the blend mode of the top layer to Screen. Because screen is a lightening blend mode it has the effect of lightening the entire photo.

TIP: You can use the keyboard shortcut Option-Shift-S (PC: Alt-Shift-S) to switch to the Screen blend mode quickly.

STEP 3: REDUCE THE OPACITY OR ERASE AWAY ANY AREAS THAT ARE TOO LIGHT

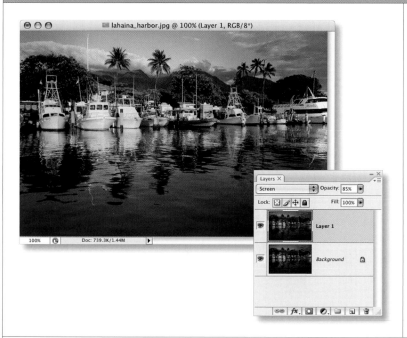

Since we duplicated our layer in this example, we can always go back and reduce the opacity of the Screen layer, or we can use the Eraser tool (E) to erase away any areas from it that became too light.

STEP 4: PROBLEM: FADED PHOTOS. OPEN A FADED PHOTO AND DUPLICATE THE BACKGROUND

Another problem that blend modes can help is when you have a faded or dull photo. Here I've opened an old photo of my grandparents. As you can see, most of it is faded. The first step is to duplicate the Background layer by pressing Command-J (PC: Ctrl-J).

CARL ZUMBANO

STEP 5: CHANGE THE BLEND MODE TO MULTIPLY. ERASE ANY AREAS THAT BECAME TOO DARK

Change the blend mode of the duplicate layer to Multiply. Since Multiply is a darkening blend mode, this has the effect of darkening everything in the photo. It may look just fine like that, so feel free to leave it alone. However, if you've darkened an area too much (here I think her dress and hair became too dark) just use the Eraser tool (E) on the duplicate layer to erase it away and reveal the lighter original layer below. You may need to reduce the opacity of the Eraser tool in the Options Bar so the contrast isn't too great.

STEP 6: PROBLEM: BRIGHT SKY AND DARK FOREGROUND

The last problem we're going to take a look at is when you have a photo with a bright sky and a dark foreground. This can usually be helped when taking the photo by using a graduated neutral density gradient filter on the camera. However, there are some things you can do after the fact in Photoshop to help, too. First, open the photo you want to enhance. Here's one where the sky is somewhat bright but the foreground is actually a little too dark.

STEP 7: CREATE A NEW LAYER. DRAW A BLACK-TO-WHITE GRADIENT ON IT

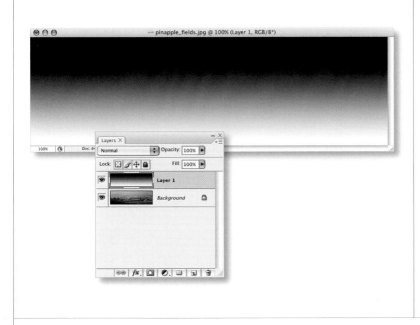

Create a new layer above the Background layer by clicking on the Create a New Layer icon at the bottom of the Layers panel. Then select the Gradient tool (G) from the Toolbox. Press Return (PC: Enter) to bring up the Gradient Picker. It'll show up wherever your cursor is on the screen. Then, choose the third gradient from the top left. It's one of the default gradients called Black, White. Finally, make sure you select the Linear Gradient option (the first icon to the right of the gradient thumbnail) in the Options Bar. Now, click-and-drag the gradient from the top of the photo to the bottom.

Remember those contrast-enhancing blend modes? They come in really handy here because we want to blend based on the color of the gradient. Where the gradient is black, I want the photo below to be darkened, and where the gradient is white, I want it to be lightened. To make this happen, change the layer blend mode to Overlay, and drop the Opacity a little. You'll see the overall photo looks much better.

TIP: Experiment with the Soft Light blend mode for this, too. It's a little more subtle and sometimes it looks better on photos with a lot of colorful areas in them.

ADVANCED LAYER BLENDING

THERE'S ONE MORE ASPECT OF LAYER BLENDING THAT'LL REALLY KNOCK YOUR SOCKS OFF

There's one area of blending layers that we haven't looked at yet called Blending Options. Trust me, it's *way* different than anything you've seen before. See, blend modes fade parts of your image based on the colors in them, but you really don't have any control over what gets blended. There's a preset formula for a blend mode and it will always follow that formula. The blending options, on the other hand, let you control exactly which parts of the photo get blended.

STEP 1: OPEN TWO IMAGES THAT YOU'D LIKE TO BLEND TOGETHER

Open two images that you'd like to blend together. Here, we'll use a photo of a sunset and a photo of a moon. We want to blend the moon into the sunset and behind the palm trees without making all of those complex selections that you'd normally start thinking of when you look at this project.

STEP 2: MOVE THE MOON PHOTO INTO THE SAME DOCUMENT AS THE SUNSET

To kick things off, get the Move tool (V) and click-and-drag the photo of the moon into the same document as the photo of the sunset. Position it over the middle of the sunset photo on top of some palm trees. The moon layer should be on top of the original sunset photo in the Layers panel.

STEP 3: OPEN THE BLENDING OPTIONS FOR THE MOON LAYER

To merge these two images together, we'll use the Layers panel's Blending Options layer style. Click on the Add a Layer Style icon at the bottom of the Layers panel and choose Blending Options from the pop-up menu.

TIP: You can double-click on the layer as a shortcut to open the Blending Options section of the Layer Style dialog.

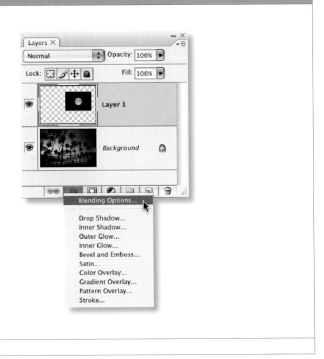

STEP 4: DRAG THE TOP-LEFT BLEND IF SLIDER TO DROP OUT THE BLACK IN THE MOON IMAGE

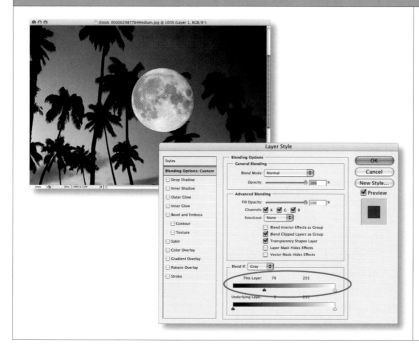

We'll do this in two phases: First, let's get rid of the black background around the moon. Drag the black This Layer Blend If slider (the top-left slider) toward the right and you'll see the black background start to drop out. I dragged mine to 78. If you drag too far to the right, you'll actually start to drop out some of the gray colors in the moon. If that happens, just drag the slider back toward the left until just the black around the moon is gone. If you're wondering how this is all happening, then check out the next step. If not, then skip to Step 6 to finish the project.

STEP 5: WHAT THE HECK IS GOING ON?

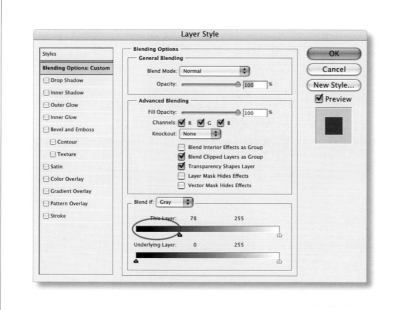

All right, if you're one of those who has to know how and why this is happening, here's the deal: the Blend If sliders tell Photoshop to blend certain color values if a layer's values fall within a certain range. In the example in the previous step, we told Photoshop to blend the moon layer if any color values from this layer (which is the one we've selected in the Layers panel) fall between 0 and 78. Remember, 78 is where we set the slider. If you look at the dialog here, you'll see the colors that are circled are the ones blended (mostly black).

Right now the image doesn't look very realistic with the moon in front of the trees. We could always just move the moon over an open sky area, but that would be lame, right? So, let's bring the trees in. Click-and-drag the black Underlying Layer Blend If slider (the bottom-left one) toward the right to reveal the trees behind the moon. I dragged mine to 85. If you go too far, you'll start to hide the moon, so pull back. This tells Photoshop to blend the moon layer if the pixels from the underlying layer (the sunset photo) are equal to or darker than the value you dragged the slider to (85).

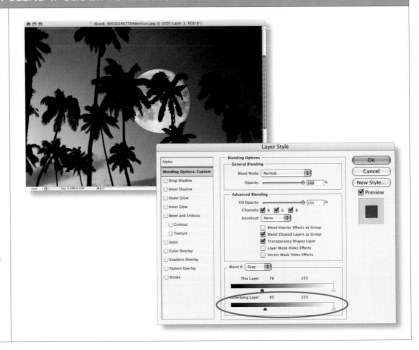

Ready for the kicker? The one thing that brings this all together? If you zoom in (press Z to get the Zoom tool), you'll see the edges of the trees around the moon look really ragged. It's the one tell-tale sign that we've "faked" this image. To fix it, press-and-hold the Option (PC: Alt) key and click-and-drag the black Underlying Layer slider to the left. This splits the slider and tells Photoshop to fade any colors between the two ends of the sliders. Take the slider over to 12 or so and you'll see the edges of the tree look 100% better around the moon. Click OK and you're done. Sweet, huh? Best of all, no painful selections were made in this process.

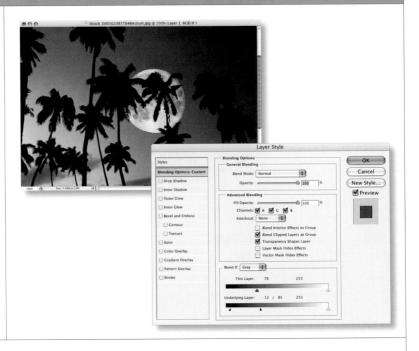

HOW DO I...

? CHANGE A LAYER'S BLEND MODE?

Click on the layer to select it, then click on the blend mode pop-up menu in the top left of the Layers panel and choose your blend mode.

? CYCLE THROUGH ALL OF THE BLEND MODES WITH THE KEYBOARD?

Click on the blend mode pop-up menu in the top left of the Layers panel to select a blend mode. Then press Shift–+ (plus sign) to cycle down the menu and Shift– - (minus sign) to go back up.

? OPEN THE LAYER STYLE DIALOG WITH LAYER BLENDING OPTIONS?

Double-click on the layer in the Layers panel.

? QUICKLY CHANGE TO THE MULTIPLY BLEND MODE?

Press Option-Shift-M (PC: Alt-Shift-M).

? QUICKLY CHANGE TO THE SCREEN BLEND MODE?

Press Option-Shift-S (PC: Alt-Shift-S).

? QUICKLY CHANGE TO THE SOFT LIGHT BLEND MODE?

Press Option-Shift-F (PC: Alt-Shift-F).

? CHANGE LAYER OPACITY WITH THE KEYBOARD?

Quickly type the first number of the layer opacity setting you want. For 50%, type 5. For 35%, quickly type 35. (To use this keyboard shortcut, be sure you don't have a tool selected that has a percentage setting in the Options Bar.)

CHAPTER THREE

ADJUSTMENT LAYERS

At this point, you've seen how useful layers are for making adjustments to your images. But we've only been working with regular layers. There's also something in Photoshop called an adjustment layer. It's a different type of layer that has really changed the way people edit their images, because they let you work non-destructively. Even better, adjustment layers let you apply adjustments to selective parts of your photos so you don't have to apply the adjustments to the whole image—just part of it, if you want. They're way cool and they're easy to start using.

ADJUSTMENT LAYER BASICS

ADJUSTMENT LAYERS GIVE US THE ULTIMATE FLEXIBILITY WHEN IT COMES TO MAKING OUR PHOTOS LOOK BETTER

Why are adjustment layers so cool? Let's say we have a photo that we'd like to turn into a black-and-white photo. Sure, you can use the Black & White adjustment under the Image>Adjustments menu, but when you apply it to your image, you've made a permanent change. So if you save the file, you'd never be able to go back and see your color image again. Well, most of those adjustments under the Image>Adjustments menu are also available as an adjustment layer. These little layers do the same exact adjustment, but on a separate layer. Not only can you easily get back to your original image by using adjustment layers, but you can also easily change the settings if you change your mind later on.

STEP 1: OPEN A PHOTO OF AN OBJECT WHOSE COLOR YOU'D LIKE TO CHANGE

There are a ton of examples to use for adjustment layers. Let's start out by changing the color of an object in a photo. So, go ahead and open a photo that has something you'd like to change the color of. In this example, we'll use a daisy. (*Note:* If you want to follow along using this daisy image, you can download it from the website mentioned in the introduction.)

©ISTOCKPHOTO/LISA THORNBERG

Just so you can see where these adjustment layers are coming from, click on the Image menu and look under Adjustments. See all of the options there? These are the various color and tonal corrections that are available in Photoshop. Some of the most popular ones are Levels, Curves, Hue/Saturation, and Color Balance.

Now, let's compare that Adjustments submenu with the adjustment layers pop-up menu. Go over to the Layers panel. Look at the very bottom for the little half-black/half-white circle icon. This is the Create New Adjustment Layer icon. Click on it and look at the options in the pop-up menu. Notice how most of them are the same exact ones that were under the Image>Adjustments submenu?

STEP 4: ADD A HUE/SATURATION ADJUSTMENT

Since you're already there, choose Hue/Saturation from the pop-up menu to add a Hue/Saturation adjustment layer. You'll see the Hue/Saturation dialog open. Drag the Hue setting to –32. That changes the color of the daisy to orange.

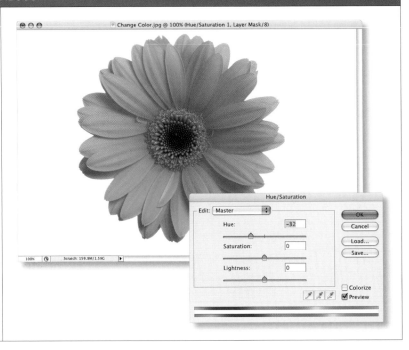

STEP 5: CLICK OK, THEN LOOK IN THE LAYERS PANEL TO SEE THE NEW LAYER

Once you've settled on a color, click OK to close the Hue/Saturation dialog. Then look over in the Layers panel. There's a new layer above the Background layer. That's an adjustment layer. The adjustment has essentially been applied to a separate layer, not the original photo. You can see this by looking closely at the Background layer thumbnail—the daisy is still yellow in the thumbnail, even though it looks orange onscreen.

STEP 6: HIDE THE ADJUSTMENT LAYER TO SEE THE ORIGINAL

Adjustment layers work a lot like regular layers do. They have an opacity setting, you can rename them, and you can even hide them. Try it. Click on the little Eye icon to the left of the adjustment layer's thumbnail and now you'll see your original photo that is underneath it in the Layers panel. The original yellow color is all safe and sound.

STEP 7: SAVE THE LAYERED FILE AND REOPEN IT LATER. EDIT THE ADJUSTMENT LAYER

Let's assume you're done working. Save this image in the Photoshop PSD format under the File>Save As menu. Now, participate in a little role-playing game with me for a moment. Assume you show this to a client and they say they'd prefer a red daisy instead. All you have to do is open the same PSD file and double-click on the Hue/Saturation adjustment layer's thumbnail to re-open the dialog. Photoshop remembers the settings you entered last time. To modify them, just drag the Hue slider to, say, −54 to change the color to red. Click OK and you're set. With adjustment layers you've always got a way out and a way to go back and change the settings.

MAKING SELECTIVE ADJUSTMENTS

IT DOESN'T HAVE TO BE ALL OR NOTHING WITH ADJUSTMENT LAYERS. YOU CAN SELECTIVELY CHANGE THINGS TOO!

Hey, what you just saw in the previous tutorial is pretty darn cool. Always having the ability to go and edit your adjustments at a later date is very powerful stuff. However, let's face it. The all or nothing factor of an adjustment layer can be limiting. Let's say that you have a photo where the sky looks great but the foreground is just too dark. You can always add a Levels adjustment layer to brighten the foreground but it's going to brighten the sky too. Probably to the point where it's too bright, right? However, with adjustment layers you can selectively make adjustments to certain areas in your photos without affecting the whole thing.

STEP 1: OPEN A PHOTO WHERE ONLY ONE AREA NEEDS TO BE FIXED

Open a photo where one part of the photo looks fine but another area needs some work. In this case, I have a landscape photo. The foreground looks too dark, but the sky looks fine.

STEP 2: ADD A LEVELS ADJUSTMENT LAYER TO BRIGHTEN THE FOREGROUND

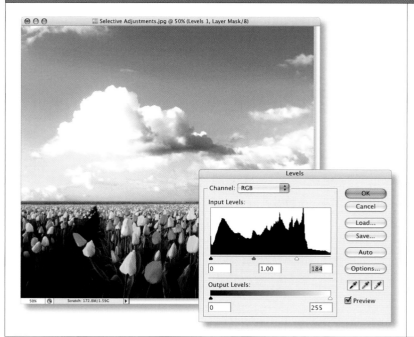

Go to the bottom of the Layers panel and click on the Create New Adjustment Layer icon. From the pop-up menu, choose Levels. Now drag the white Input Levels slider toward the left to brighten the foreground. Notice how the foreground area gets brighter, but the clouds and the sky get way too bright. In fact, we lose a lot of the detail in the clouds when we do this. Go ahead and click Cancel to close the dialog so we can make a quick change.

STEP 3: MAKE A SELECTION OF THE AREA YOU WANT TO BRIGHTEN FIRST

So, you've seen what happens when you just apply the Levels adjustment to the whole photo. This time, grab the Rectangular Marquee tool (M) and make a selection of the area you want to modify. Here, it's the tulips in the foreground. Just click-and-drag around the bottom part of the photo with the Rectangular Marquee tool to make the selection.

Go back and add a Levels adjustment layer again. Drag the white Input Levels slider over toward the left just like you did before. I've dragged mine until the white point reads 171. Notice how only the area you selected in Step 3 gets brighter (the bottom tulips in this example)? The sky doesn't change. Go ahead and click OK when you're happy with the way the adjustment looks.

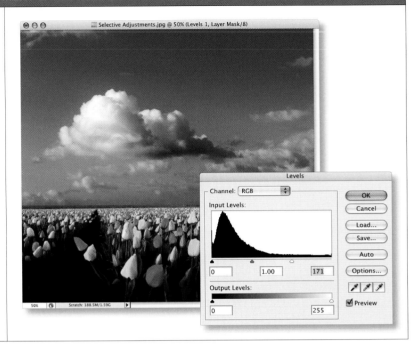

So, how did this happen? What's the deal? Well, take a look at that little white-and-black thumbnail next to the Levels adjustment layer thumbnail in the Layers panel. This is a layer mask (it's circled in red here). If you recall from the previous tutorial, when we changed the color of the daisy with a Hue/Saturation adjustment, that layer mask was all white. Here's a screen capture of the Layers panel from the previous tutorial and the one from our example here to compare. See how the one from the earlier tutorial is all white, but the one from this tutorial shows white only in the area we made a selection on?

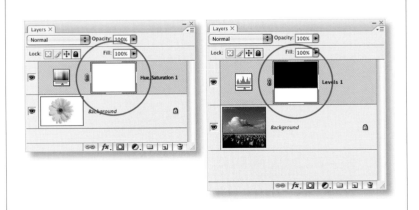

STEP 6: BLACK HIDES THE ADJUSTMENT AND SHOWS THE LAYER THAT IS DIRECTLY UNDERNEATH IT

The main thing to remember here is that the color (black or white) that you see on the little thumbnail actually matters. When it's all white, we see the effects of the adjustment layer over the entire photo. Wherever it's black, though, the effects of the adjustment layer get hidden and the original photo underneath the adjustment layer will show through. So, here the white is our selection of the ground and shows us our Levels adjustment, while the black is over the sky area and shows us the sky from the Background layer.

STEP 7: NOW OPEN AN IMAGE WHERE THE HORIZON ISN'T PERFECTLY STRAIGHT

I'll admit it. I picked a "gimme" photo in that last example. How often are your horizons perfectly straight like that, right? It was a good example to start with, but let's take it further. What happens when the horizon isn't as perfectly horizontal as the last image was? Open another photo that may take a little more effort than just a quick selection with the Rectangular Marquee tool.

STEP 8: THIS TIME, MAKE A SELECTION THAT COVERS MOST OF THE AREA YOU WANT TO FIX

Just like last time, grab the Rectangular Marquee tool (M) and make a selection of the foreground. Don't worry if the selection extends into the sky, though. We can fix it later.

STEP 9: ADD A LEVELS ADUSTMENT LAYER TO BRIGHTEN THE FOREGROUND

Add a Levels adjustment layer. Click-and-drag the white Input Levels slider to the left to brighten the bottom of the photo. You may also want to experiment with the gray and black Input Levels sliders to give it a little color boost as well as contrast. Click OK when you're done.

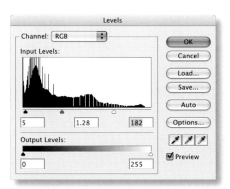

STEP 10: LOOK AT THE PHOTO TO SEE WHERE THE ADJUSTMENT SPILLED OVER INTO THE SKY

At this point you'll have a new Levels adjustment layer in the Layers panel. Take a look at the photo, though, and you'll see that the brightened area of the Levels adjustment actually spills over into the sky. That's because you selected that part of the sky before adding the Levels adjustment layer. So the adjustment layer just looks at whatever was selected and brightens it regardless of whether you wanted to or not. No problem—we can fix it after the fact.

STEP 11: MAKE A SELECTION OF THE PARTS OF THE SKY THAT SHOULDN'T BE BRIGHTER

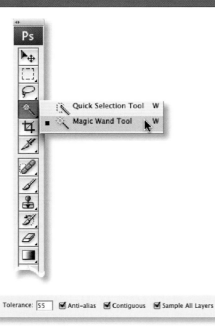

In order to fix the sky and bring it back to the way it was, you'll need to make another selection. Select the Magic Wand tool (press Shift-W until you have it). For this photo, set the tolerance to 55 and make sure that the Contiguous and Sample All Layers checkboxes are turned on in the Options Bar up top.

TIP: If you have Photoshop CS3, there's a new selection tool called the Quick Selection tool, nested with the Magic Wand tool. I'm totally addicted to it and it works wonders on selections like this one, so give it a try.

STEP 12: USE THE MAGIC WAND TOOL TO SELECT THE AREA IN THE SKY THAT IS TOO BRIGHT

Click on the area in the sky that's too bright to select it. If you don't get all of the area with one click, then press-and-hold the Shift key and keep clicking in the areas that remain to select them, as well.

STEP 13: FILL THE SELECTED AREA ON THE LEVELS ADJUSTMENT LAYER WITH BLACK

Click once on the Levels adjustment layer's mask thumbnail to make it active. In order to make it so the sky looks like it did when we first started, you've got to fill the selection with black to match the rest of the black area on that black-and-white thumbnail. So click on the Edit menu and choose Fill. From the Use pop-up menu, choose Black. Click OK to fill the selection. Then choose Select>Deselect (or press Command-D [PC: Ctrl-D]) to deselect all.

STEP 14: DOUBLE-CLICK THE LEVELS ADJUSTMENT TO EDIT THE SETTINGS, IF NEEDED

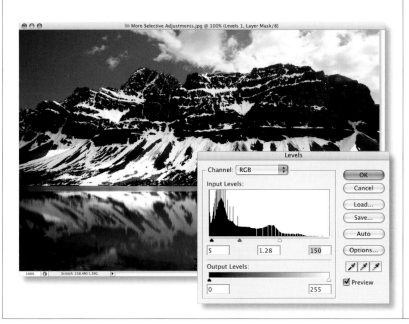

The sky should look just like it did when you started. The Levels adjustment will only affect the foreground area. However, after seeing the final image, it looks like we can make the foreground a little brighter. To edit the Levels adjustment, double-click on the adjustment layer's thumbnail in the Layers panel. This will reopen the Levels dialog. To lighten the foreground more, drag the white Input Levels slider toward the left. See how the adjustment is still only affecting part of the photo, though? It only shows on the part that's white in that layer mask next to the adjustment layer thumbnail.

STEP 15: CLICK OK TO CLOSE THE DIALOG. TOGGLE THE ADJUSTMENT LAYER ON AND OFF

Go ahead and click OK to close the Levels dialog. You can click the little Eye icon to the left of the Levels adjustment layer to hide the adjustment effects and look at the before image. Then click where the Eye icon was to show the adjustment.

Before   *After*

SUPER FLEXIBLE ADJUSTMENTS

OKAY, NOW FOR THE REALLY COOL STUFF. ADJUSTMENT LAYERS HAVE ONE MORE SUPER COOL, FLEXIBLE FEATURE

So far you've seen that adjustment layers can stand on their own and apply an adjustment to the entire layer. You've seen that you can make a selection to restrict the areas that an adjustment layer can affect. And you've even learned how to tweak that selection after the fact if you need to. It doesn't stop there, though. Adjustment layers have one more super cool, flexible feature to work with: brushes. Selections are great, but sometimes they're a pain to create the way that you want them—especially if you have a difficult-to-select area. By using a brush on the adjustment layer, you can specifically apply the adjustment to the exact areas you want by painting them with black instead of filling a selection with black. It's the same concept but *way* more controlled and *way* easier.

STEP 1: OPEN A PHOTO THAT NEEDS AN ADJUSTMENT IN A SPECIFIC AREA

Open a photo that needs an adjustment in a specific area. In this case, the couple seems to be in the shadows and doesn't really stand out from the background in the photo.

TIP: As you can see, I'm using a photo of people for this example. This could just as easily be a landscape photo similar to the ones we've looked at in this chapter, where some portion of the foreground is too dark and you want to lighten it. Just thought I'd mention that. You can read on now.

MATT KLOSKOWSKI

STEP 2: ADD A CURVES ADJUSTMENT LAYER TO BRIGHTEN THE PHOTO

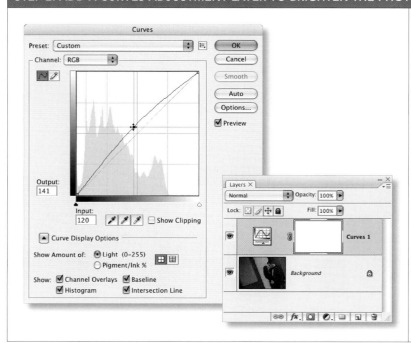

This time around, let's add a Curves adjustment layer to brighten the couple. Click on the Create New Adjustment Layer icon at the bottom of the Layers panel, and choose Curves from the pop-up menu. Click in the middle of the diagonal line (the curve) and drag it upward and to the left. If you're not sure how far upward to drag right now, it's totally fine because we can come back and adjust it later. Click OK when you're done to add the adjustment layer. You'll see the new Curves adjustment layer appear in the Layers panel above the Background layer.

STEP 3: SELECT THE BRUSH TOOL AND CHOOSE A SEMI-LARGE, SOFT-EDGED BRUSH

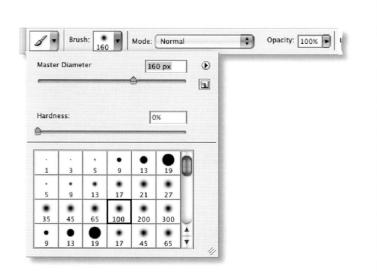

Now, the whole photo got brighter as a result of the Curves adjustment. What we really want is for the couple to be brighter and the rest of the image the way it was. To make this happen, let's paint with black on the adjustment layer over the background to bring back the original dark photo in certain areas. First, select the Brush tool (B) from the Toolbox. Click on the brush thumbnail up in the Options Bar, and choose a large, soft-edged brush from the Brush Picker. Make sure your Foreground color is set to black (if black is your background color instead, press X to switch them).

STEP 4: PAINT ON THE BACKGROUND BEHIND THE COUPLE TO DARKEN IT

Click once on the Curves adjustment layer's mask thumbnail to
make sure it's active (you'll see a
thin black frame around the corners). Start clicking-and-dragging
on the background in the photo
with the Brush tool. Normally, this
would paint black on the photo.
However, we're working on the
layer mask, so it's different. This
paints black on the layer mask
next to the Curves adjustment
layer thumbnail. By painting with
black, you'll be bringing back the
original background from the layer
under the Curves adjustment layer
(which was darker, by the way). If
you mess up, just press X to switch
your Foreground color to white,
and paint over the mistake.

STEP 5: CONTINUE PAINTING ON THE LAYER MASK UNTIL ALL THE BACKGROUND IS DARK AGAIN

Continue to paint until all of the
background area looks darker
again. You can always look at
the layer mask thumbnail on the
Curves adjustment layer to get a
glimpse of any white areas that
may still be left. You may also need
to zoom in and reduce your brush
size as you get close to the faces
and edges of the couple so you
can be more precise. This works
just like the previous tutorial did
except we're painting with black
instead of filling a selection with
black. Photoshop doesn't care how
you get black on the layer mask,
though. As long as it's black, the
original layer under the adjustment
layer will show through.

STEP 6: DOUBLE-CLICK THE ADJUSTMENT LAYER THUMBNAIL TO TWEAK THE CURVE

Finally, remember how we weren't sure how much to drag the curve back in Step 2? You can always double-click on the Curves adjustment layer thumbnail in the Layers panel and tweak the curve more. Since you've already done the work of hiding the Curves adjustment from the background so it only affects the couple, any changes you make to the curve will be like turning a light brighter or darker on the couple. You can see exactly how much you want them to stand out from the background. I told you this stuff was cool!

Before

After

SOME MORE ADJUSTMENT LAYER IDEAS

ONCE YOU START USING ADJUSTMENT LAYERS, IT'S HARD TO STOP. HERE ARE A FEW MORE IDEAS

Trust me, once you start using adjustment layers a whole new world of creative possibilities opens up. In fact, just about everything you do to fix or enhance your photos touches something up in that Image>Adjustments menu. So, why not go ahead and use an adjustment layer for it instead? Here, I'll show you some quick examples of adjustment layers.

EXAMPLE 1: STEP 1: CREATING A BLACK-AND-WHITE IMAGE

This one is a cakewalk, but there are a few different options. One really popular technique is taking a color photo and making it a black-and-white. There are three ways to do this using adjustment layers: (1) add a Hue/Saturation adjustment and move the Saturation slider all the way to the left, (2) add a Channel Mixer adjustment, and (3) if you have Photoshop CS3, just use the new Black & White adjustment.

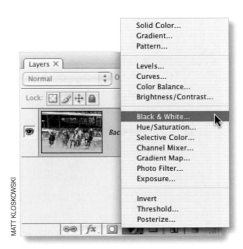

STEP 2: GIVE CHANNEL MIXER A TRY

First off, option (1) totally stinks so don't use it. It creates a flat, dull black-and-white image, so forget I even mentioned it. Before Photoshop CS3, most people preferred the Channel Mixer method for creating black-and-whites. So open a photo that you want to convert to black and white and add a Channel Mixer adjustment layer. Then turn on the Monochrome checkbox and your photo will turn to black and white just like that. Feel free to adjust the sliders to change the way certain colors (reds, greens, and blues) appear in the photo. Moving to the left will make them darker and moving to the right will make them lighter.

STEP 3: IF YOU'VE GOT CS3, THEN TRY THE BLACK & WHITE ADJUSTMENT

If you have Photoshop CS3, then the new Black & White adjustment has pretty much replaced the Channel Mixer method. It has a lot more flexibility to create great black-and-whites. Once you open a photo to convert, add a Black & White adjustment layer. Here you can affect each color in the photo individually by dragging its associated slider. Say the sky looks too dark. Try dragging the Blue slider to the right to lighten it. If it's too light, just drag it to the left to darken it. The same thing works for the other colors.

EXAMPLE 2: STEP 1: ENHANCING SUNRISE OR SUNSET SKIES WITH A GRADIENT MAP

One adjustment we haven't talked about yet is the gradient map. This one works great for enhancing skies in sunrise or sunset photos. Open a photo of a good sunrise or sunset. Then add a Gradient Map adjustment layer. When the Gradient Map dialog opens, click on the gradient thumbnail in the middle to open the Gradient Editor. Then double-click on the two color stops below the gradient ramp (near the bottom of the dialog) to add your own colors. It works best when you add two colors that are similar to colors in the sky (red and yellow here).

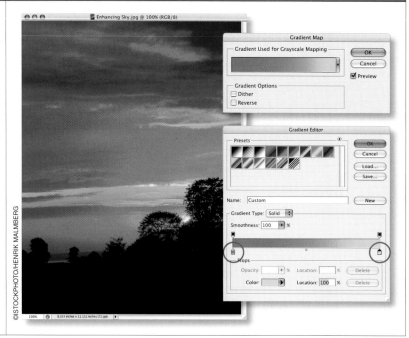

STEP 2: CHANGE THE ADJUSTMENT LAYER'S BLEND MODE TO COLOR

Click OK twice to lock in the adjustment. Finally, change the blend mode of the adjustment layer to Color.

EXAMPLE 3: SELECTIVELY ADDING COLOR

Here's another popular technique: you can create a black-and-white photo and then selectively add back color. It's great for really drawing someone in to look at the subject and makes for a very dramatic effect. First, use your favorite black-and-white conversion method from the first example in this tutorial. Here I've used the Black & White adjustment layer. Then paint with a black brush on the areas you want to bring back into color. In this example, the butterfly is the subject and we'll paint on its wings to show the color again. I just love this technique!

EXAMPLE 4: STEP 1: CHANGING THE MOOD OR FEEL OF A PHOTO

The Photo Filter adjustment layer is great for totally changing the mood or feel of a photo. It simulates the effect of traditional warming and cooling filters that used to be attached to the end of a lens. In this example, just open a photo that needs a little something extra. Then add a Photo Filter adjustment layer. Choose one of the warming filters to enhance the effect of that great early morning light.

Another option with the Photo Filter adjustment on the previous page is to use a cooling filter. This has the opposite effect of the warming filter. It tends to make a photo appear very cool. Look how it totally changes the mood and feel in this photo and makes it appear very cold.

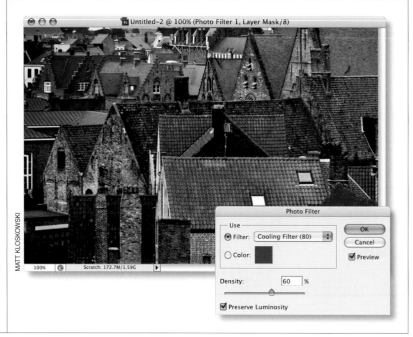

EXAMPLE 5: SPLIT TONING EFFECT

Split toning is an effect where you apply a color tint to the shadows in a photo and then another color tint to the highlights (splitting the tones). It's a cool effect for a photo and really easy to do with adjustment layers. First, add a Black & White adjustment layer. Then add a Color Balance adjustment layer on top of it. When the Color Balance dialog opens, click on the Highlights radio button at the bottom. For this example, drag the Yellow/Blue (bottom) slider to –16. That tones the highlights. Then click on the Shadows radio button and drag the Red/Cyan (top) slider to +35. Click OK when you're done.

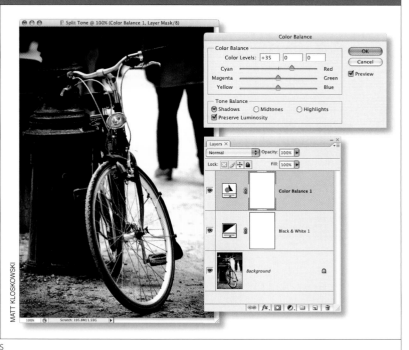

FIX ONE PHOTO—FIX 'EM ALL!

NOT ONLY ARE ADJUSTMENT LAYERS FLEXIBLE, BUT THEY CAN ALSO SAVE YOU A TON OF TIME

I flat-out love features that save me time. So far, I've been showing you how adjustment layers are great, wonderful, flexible, and all that stuff. Put all that aside for a minute, though, and take a look at a technique with adjustment layers that'll save you a ton of time if you're working on a bunch of photos that were shot in similar conditions.

STEP 1: OPEN ONE PHOTO FROM A GROUP OF PHOTOS THAT NEED ADJUSTING

Open a photo that was taken with a group of photos that need adjusting. Here's an underwater photo of a boy in a swimming pool. It's a great shot, but the underwater nature of the photo makes it way too green. Plus, it's a little flat, so it can use a little contrast boost.

©FOTOLIA/CELESTE DAVIDSON

STEP 2: ADD A CURVES ADJUSTMENT LAYER

Click on the Create New Adjustment Layer icon at the bottom of the Layers panel and choose Curves to add a Curves adjustment layer. First, let's give the photo a little more punch. Click on the bottom half of the curve, and drag it downward, then click-and-drag upward in the top half, as shown here. This gives it that classic S-curve shape and gives the photo better contrast overall.

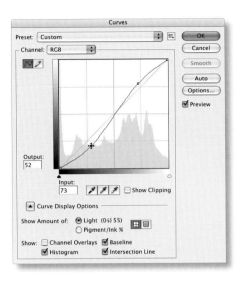

STEP 3: SWITCH TO THE RED CHANNEL AND ADD SOME RED

Because the photo was taken underwater, it's got a strong green/blue color cast to it. Since red is the opposite of green, adding more red to the photo should neutralize some of the green. Click on the Channel pop-up menu at the top and choose Red. Then click in the middle of the curve and drag it upward to add some red to the photo. Click OK when you're done.

STEP 4: OPEN ANOTHER PHOTO THAT WAS SHOT IN SIMILAR CONDITIONS

©FOTOLIA/CELESTE DAVIDSON

Cool! You've adjusted one photo. However, we have a couple more photos of this boy in the pool that we need to fix. We don't want to go in and re-create that Curves adjustment layer for each photo. Not a problem. Just open the other photos that were shot in the same conditions. As you can see, they all suffer from the same green color cast and lack of contrast.

STEP 5: DRAG THE ADJUSTMENT LAYER OVER TO THE OTHER PHOTOS

Remember that adjustment layers are just like all the other layers in the Layers panel. That means you can click-and-drag them onto another photo just like you can a layer. So, position the photo we just fixed and one of the other photos that needs fixing so you can see them both. Click on the Curves adjustment layer in the Layers panel and drag it over one of the photos that needs fixing. That copies the adjustment layer and all of its settings over to the other photo. With just one quick drag of a layer, you've fixed that photo too.

STEP 6: TAKE IT A STEP FURTHER AND ADD SEVERAL ADJUSTMENT LAYERS

What we just did is really cool, but many times your images will require more than one adjustment. We can take this a step further by adding several adjustment layers. Here, I've added a Levels adjustment and a Color Balance adjustment to help improve the photo even more.

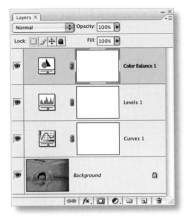

STEP 7: PUT THE ADJUSTMENT LAYERS IN A GROUP

Select all of the adjustment layers by Command-clicking (PC: Ctrl-clicking) on them. Then press Command-G (PC: Ctrl-G) to put them into a group. Now all of your adjustment layers are in one folder in the Layers panel.

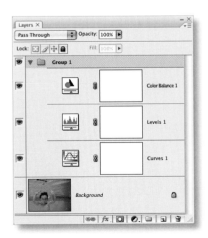

Just like you did in Step 5, position the image we just fixed, as well as one that needs fixing, so you can see both onscreen. Then click-and-drag the group from the Layers panel of our adjusted photo onto one of the photos that needs adjusting. Now all three adjustment layers are copied over at once. Then, just repeat this process for each photo that needs adjusting. It's a lot easier than adding the adjustments to each photo individually.

THE ADJUSTMENT LAYER BLEND MODE TRICK

YOU DON'T HAVE TO DO ANYTHING TO AN ADJUSTMENT LAYER TO MAKE IT USEFUL

Okay, I'm going to get a little techie on you here. But trust me, I'm doing it for your own good. I'm getting techie because it'll help you be more creative in the long run—you'll see why. Many times, when you're working on a layered document you'll duplicate a layer and change its blend mode to something like Multiply or Screen just like we did in Chapter 2. Then you'll selectively erase part of that duplicate layer (or better yet, use layer masks, which we'll talk more about in the next chapter). Here's the thing: the second you duplicate that layer, your image is taking up twice as much space on your computer as it did before.

STEP 1: IF YOU BELIEVE ME, THEN SKIP TO STEP 2. IF NOT, THEN TRY A QUICK TEST

If you read the intro and you believe how much space just one duplicate copy of a layer takes up, then go ahead and skip to Step 2. If you don't believe me, then try a quick test. Open a photo right from your camera. In my case, I shoot with a 10-megapixel camera in RAW mode, so here's one of the photos opened in Photoshop. I saved it to the desktop when it had just one layer. Then I duplicated the Background layer and saved another copy to the desktop when it had two layers. When compared, the image with two layers was a whopping 46 MB larger than the image with one layer. Enough said?

MATT KLOSKOWSKI

STEP 2: OPEN A PHOTO THAT WOULD BENEFIT FROM ONE OF THE BLEND MODE TUTORIALS IN CHAPTER 2

Go ahead and open a photo that would benefit from one of the blend modes (Screen or Multiply) discussed in Chapter 2. In this photo, I think the boat is too dark and just kind of blends into the background. The whole image would look a lot better if the boat were lighter against a dark background.

STEP 3: ADD A LEVELS OR CURVES ADJUSTMENT LAYER, BUT THIS TIME DON'T CHANGE THE SETTINGS

Add a Levels or Curves adjustment layer on top of the Background layer by clicking on the Create New Adjustment Layer icon at the bottom of the Layers panel. It doesn't really matter which one you use, since we're not actually going to change the settings. Just add the adjustment layer, and when the dialog appears, click OK to accept the default (no change) settings.

STEP 4: CHANGE THE BLEND MODE OF THE ADJUSTMENT LAYER TO SCREEN

Change the blend mode of the adjustment layer to Screen. This will lighten the entire image onscreen. What's important to note here is that this change has the same exact effect as duplicating the Background layer and changing its blend mode to Screen.

STEP 5: USE THE BRUSH TOOL TO REVEAL ANY OF THE ORIGINAL LAYER BELOW

Now switch to the Brush tool (B) and make sure your Foreground color is set to Black (if your Background color swatch is black, press X to switch the colors). Here, I chose a 200-pixel, soft-edged brush from the Brush Picker. Then, I made sure the little white thumbnail (layer mask) was selected in the Layers panel and painted over the background to reveal the darker areas below and just show the screened effect on the boat. It made the boat really stand out more. When saved as a PSD file, the file size is considerably smaller than it was with two layers. Smaller file size means less hard drive space used, less RAM used, and overall less processing power needed for your image.

HOW DO I...

Just like you would any other layer: press Command-J (PC: Ctrl-J).

? RESET THE SETTINGS INSIDE AN ADJUSTMENT LAYER'S DIALOG?

To reset your settings when you're in an adjustment layer's dialog, press-and-hold the Option (PC: Alt) key and the Cancel button will change to a Reset button.

? PREVIEW THE BEFORE/AFTER EFFECTS OF THE ADJUSTMENT LAYER WHILE IN THE DIALOG?

Turn the Preview checkbox on and off.

? SET MY FOREGROUND/BACKGROUND COLORS TO THEIR DEFAULTS (BLACK AND WHITE) FOR PAINTING WITH THE BRUSH TOOL?

Press the letter D to set your Foreground and Background colors to their defaults (black for the Foreground color and white for the Background color). These may be reversed on an adjustment layer.

? QUICKLY FILL A LAYER MASK OR SELECTION ON A LAYER MASK WITH THE FOREGROUND COLOR?

Set your Foreground color to the desired color by pressing D for the defaults or clicking on the Foreground color swatch at the bottom of the Toolbox and choosing a color from the Color Picker. Then, press Option-Delete (PC: Alt-Backspace) to fill the layer mask or selection.

? QUICKLY FILL A LAYER MASK OR SELECTION ON A LAYER MASK WITH THE BACKGROUND COLOR?

Set your Background color to the desired color by pressing D for the defaults or clicking on the Background color swatch at the bottom of the Toolbox and choosing a color from the Color Picker. Then, press Command-Delete (PC: Ctrl-Backspace) to fill the layer mask or selection.

CHAPTER FOUR

LAYER MASKS

I'm going to start this chapter intro out with a bold statement. In fact, if there's one chapter intro you want to make sure you read, it's this one. Okay, so are you ready for my bold statement? Because if you're not, I'll wait a moment—no, really, it's okay. Okay, I guess I'd better make my bold statement before I just flat out annoy you. Here it is: you already know what a layer mask is. Yep, as long as you read through and understood what we did with adjustment layers in Chapter 3, you already know all about layer masks. If you didn't read Chapter 3, then I take my bold statement back. You have no idea what a layer mask is. But you will, if you go back and read Chapter 3 and then follow it up with this chapter. Why? Because layer masks are one of the most important things you can learn when it comes to layers. It's a topic usually avoided like the bird flu. But, once you figure them out, you'll wonder how you ever got along without them.

LAYER MASK BASICS

LAYER MASKS LET YOU NON-DESTRUCTIVELY ERASE AWAY AREAS FROM ONE LAYER TO REVEAL THE LAYERS BELOW

Let me start out by saying that if you didn't read the chapter intro on the previous page, then stop right now and go read it. I made a very profound statement there and I think it's important that you read it before continuing. If you don't, then the rest of this chapter just won't be the same for you. So go read it...now. I'll wait. Okay, you're back and I bet you feel much better about embarking on your journey to learn all about layer masks. Now, in that chapter intro, I said that you already know what a layer mask is. You do! That little white thumbnail that kept getting added next to each adjustment layer we added in Chapter 3 is a layer mask. The difference between them and what we're about to do here is that adjustment layers automatically include a layer mask with them. A regular layer does not. But, it takes just one click to get the same effect.

STEP 1: OPEN TWO PHOTOS THAT YOU'D LIKE TO COMBINE

In order to really take advantage of layer masks, you need to have at least two layers. So go ahead and open two images that you'd like to combine. You can download the images shown here from the website I mentioned in the introduction.

STEP 2: DRAG ONE OF THE IMAGES ONTO THE OTHER SO THEY'RE IN THE SAME DOCUMENT

Use the Move tool (V) to drag one photo from its document onto the other one. In this example, I'm going to drag the photo of the barrel onto the image of the James Bond–looking guy with the gun. Now that photo's document has two layers. Once you've got the photo moved, you can close the original so you're left with only the document with two layers.

STEP 3: ADD A LAYER MASK TO THE TOP LAYER

Remember back in Chapter 3, whenever you added an adjustment layer it automatically added a layer mask (that little white thumbnail) to the layer it was on? Well, ordinary layers don't work like that. They don't automatically get a layer mask with them. However, adding one is really simple. First, select the layer you want to add the mask on. In this case, it's the top layer. Then click on the Add Layer Mask icon at the bottom of the Layers panel. It's the third one from the left (shown circled here).

When you click on the Add Layer Mask icon, you'll see that Photoshop adds a little white thumbnail next to the layer thumbnail in your Layers panel. This is a layer mask. See how it looks just like the one that we saw in Chapter 3 whenever we added an adjustment layer?

Adjustment layer with mask   Regular layer with mask

Right now, we can only see the barrel photo because that layer covers the one below it. Let's combine the two photos by hiding part of the top layer so we can see the layer below it. Choose the Elliptical Marquee tool from the Toolbox (or press Shift-M until you have it). Click-and-drag out a circular selection in the middle of the canvas.

TIP: You can press-and-hold the Shift key when you're making a selection with the Elliptical Marquee tool to constrain the selection to a perfect circle. Press-and-hold the Spacebar while you're dragging to move the circle.

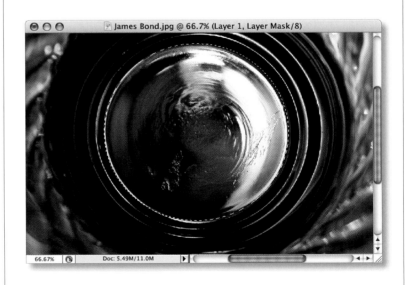

STEP 6: FILL THE SELECTION WITH BLACK

When we were working with adjustment layers, we made a selection and filled it with black to hide part of the adjustment to reveal the layer below it. The same thing works here with a regular layer mask. Go to the Edit menu and choose Fill. Then, choose Black for the Use setting and click OK. Finally, choose Select>Deselect to clear your selection.

TIP: When working on a layer mask, you can press the letter D and then the letter X to set your Foreground color to black. Then press Option-Delete (PC: Alt-Backspace) to fill any selections or layers with the Foreground color (which is black).

STEP 7: WHITE ON THE LAYER MASK SHOWS THE TOP LAYER; BLACK REVEALS THE BACKGROUND

To see how things are working here, take a look at the layer mask thumbnail. Wherever it's white, we can see the barrel layer (the layer that holds the layer mask). Where you see black on the layer mask, you see through the barrel layer to whatever is underneath it in the Layers panel (in this case, that's the James Bond–looking guy). That's probably the most important thing to understand about layer masks: black and white. White shows you the effects of the layer that the layer mask is on. Black hides the layer and shows you whatever is below it in the layer stacking order.

This layer　　　*With this Layer Mask*　　　*On top of this layer*　　=　　*This image*

STEP 8: FILL THE LAYER MASK WITH WHITE AGAIN TO GET THINGS BACK TO NORMAL

So, even though it looks like we erased away the pixels from the top barrel layer, we didn't. Instead they're just hidden from view. In real life, you'd probably save this file, then reopen it at a later time and possibly decide you want to change something. If you had erased or deleted the circular selection from the image, you'd have to go back to the original and start over. With a layer mask, though, you can always change your mind without starting over. Try it. Click on the layer mask and fill it with white this time. As you can see, all of the barrel photo is still there and the layer mask is all white again—nothing was permanently erased or deleted.

STEP 9: MAKE ANOTHER SELECTION TO CHANGE YOUR LAYER MASK

Finally, since the layer mask is still on the barrel layer, you can always make another selection and try again. This time, select the Rectangular Marquee tool (press Shift-M until you have it), make a square selection in the middle of the canvas, and fill it with black. Photoshop doesn't care what shape you create. It just cares about black and white. That's just the beginning, though. Layer masks get *way* cooler. In fact, there's a way to automatically create a layer mask. Turn to the next page to find out how.

AUTOMATICALLY CREATING LAYER MASKS

YOU CAN AUTOMATICALLY CREATE LAYER MASKS BY MAKING A SIMPLE SELECTION

The title to this tutorial definitely doesn't do it justice, but I couldn't think of a better name. It's a way to automatically create layer masks, and the amount of flexibility you get is really neat. So make sure you at least flip the page to see how cool an effect this is.

STEP 1: FIND A PHOTO WITH AN AREA IN IT THAT YOU'D LIKE TO REPLACE

Open two photos that you'd like to combine in some way. In this example, I'd like to place the photo of the airplanes inside the man's sunglasses. There's a little secret to layer masks that makes this really simple.

©ISTOCKPHOTO/ROGER LECUYER

©ISTOCKPHOTO/SERDAR YAGCI

STEP 2: SWITCH TO THE PHOTO YOU WANT TO REPLACE IT WITH, SELECT ALL, AND COPY THE PHOTO

Start off with the photo that you want to use as the replacement area. In this example, we're using the photo of the airplanes. Choose Select>All to select everything (or press Command-A [PC: Ctrl-A]), and then choose Edit>Copy (Command-C [PC: Ctrl-C]).

STEP 3: MAKE A SELECTION OF THE AREA YOU WANT TO REPLACE

Now, switch over to the photo of the man with the sunglasses on. We need to first make a selection of the area we want to replace. Here, I used the Quick Selection tool (W) to click-and-drag across the lenses inside the sunglasses to select them. If the selections spill over onto the face or the sunglasses themselves, press-and-hold the Option (PC: Alt) key and click on those areas to subtract them from the selection. If you need to add to the selection, Shift-click on the area. Press Z to get the Zoom tool if you need a larger view.

STEP 4: CHOOSE EDIT>PASTE INTO TO PASTE THE AIRPLANES INTO THE SUNGLASSES

Now click on the Edit menu and choose Paste Into (remember we copied the airplane photo in Step 2). You've probably never used this one before, but it's really cool. See, it pastes the photo you have copied (in this case, the airplanes) into the active selection. It makes sure that the photo only appears in the selection by creating a layer mask automatically. See how the name of this tutorial fits in? You've created a layer mask automatically just by using Edit>Paste Into.

STEP 5: USE THE MOVE TOOL TO REPOSITION THE PHOTO TO BETTER FIT INTO THE SUNGLASSES

Here's where it gets really cool, though: Select the Move tool from the Toolbox (or press V). Then click-and-drag the photo of the airplanes around. Photoshop lets you move the photo to reposition it, but still keeps it inside the original selection. That's because the Paste Into command created that layer mask.

STEP 6: RESIZE AND WARP THE PHOTO TO MAKE IT APPEAR MORE REALISTIC

Even better, you can resize the photo without changing anything, too. Click the Edit menu and choose Free Transform (or press Command-T [PC: Ctrl-T]). Press-and-hold the Shift key and drag one of the corner handles in to make the photo fit better. Click-and-drag inside the box to move it. Then, from the Edit menu, choose Transform>Warp. Choose Inflate from the Warp pop-up menu on the top left of the Options Bar, and bend the photo to match the distorted (bulged) perspective you'd probably see in the reflection of someone's glasses. Press Return (PC: Enter) when you're done to commit the transformation.

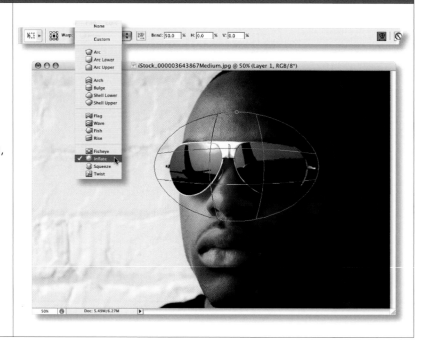

STEP 7: DROP THE OPACITY OF THE REFLECTION PHOTO TO MAKE IT BLEND IN WITH THE GLASSES

One last finishing touch would be to drop the Opacity of the airplane photo layer. This will help it blend into the sunglasses under it better. Here, I've taken the Opacity setting down to around 80%.

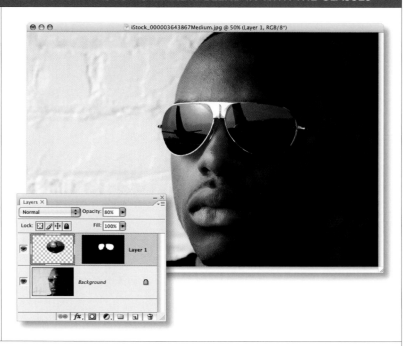

THE ONLY LAYER MASK "GOTCHA"

THERE'S ONE LITTLE DIFFERENCE YOU NEED TO KNOW ABOUT REGULAR LAYER MASKS BEFORE MOVING ON

Okay, you got me. I lied earlier. Really, it was just a tiny lie. I said earlier that there was no difference between the layer mask that was added automatically with the adjustment layer and the layer mask that you add to a regular layer. Well, that's not totally true. There is a very small difference. When we added the adjustment layers, all you had to do was click anywhere on the adjustment layer to edit its layer mask. Well, with a regular layer mask, it actually matters where you click on the layer.

STEP 1: OPEN TWO PHOTOS TO BLEND TOGETHER

First, go ahead and open two photos. They could be of anything, but I take any chance I can to show off my two sons, Ryan and Justin. Select all of one of the photos (press Command-A [PC: Ctrl-A]), then copy-and-paste it into the other one by pressing Command-C (PC: Ctrl-C), switching to the other photo, and pressing Command-V (PC: Ctrl-V), so there are now two layers in one document. With the top layer active, click on the Add Layer Mask icon at the bottom of the Layers panel to add a layer mask to the top layer.

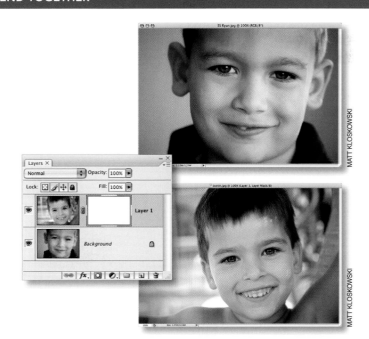

STEP 2: NOTICE THE TWO THUMBNAILS THAT APPEAR IN THE LAYERS PANEL ON THE LAYER WITH A MASK

Take a closer look at the top layer (the one with the mask). Notice how there are two thumbnails on that layer? One is the actual layer thumbnail that gives you a little preview of what is on that layer. The other is the layer mask itself.

STEP 3: CLICK ON THE LAYER THUMBNAIL TO SELECT IT

Click once on the actual layer thumbnail to select it. And I mean click on the thumbnail itself, not the highlighted area around it. If you look closely, you'll see a small black outline around the corners of the thumbnail. That's Photoshop's way of telling you that the layer is selected and ready to edit. If you were to get the Brush tool (B) and paint with black at this point, you'd be painting with black on the photo itself and you would see the black brush strokes everywhere you paint.

STEP 4: CLICK ONCE ON THE LAYER MASK THUMBNAIL TO SELECT IT

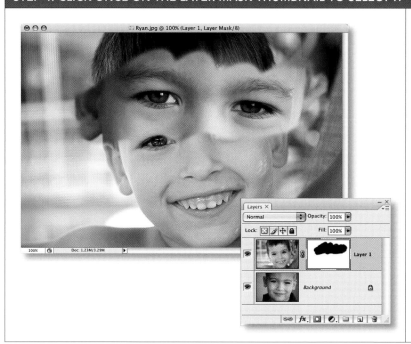

This time, click once on the layer mask thumbnail to select it. Look closely again and you'll see that black outline now appears around the corners of the layer mask, not the layer thumbnail. Now paint with a black brush on the layer mask. Wherever you paint with black, you'll start hiding the photo on that layer and revealing the layer underneath it, as you see here.

STEP 5: IT MAKES A DIFFERENCE WHAT THUMBNAIL YOU SELECT AND PAINT ON

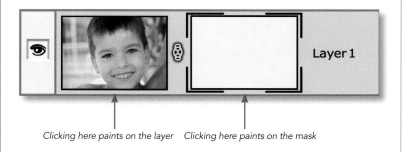

Clicking here paints on the layer   Clicking here paints on the mask

See how it makes a difference when it comes to what thumbnail you select in the Layers panel? That's why it's important to know that if you want to do something to the layer mask, you've got to actually click on that layer mask thumbnail. If you want to do something to the actual image or what you see on that layer, then click on the layer thumbnail. So, when you work with layer masks, if things aren't showing up like you thought they should, take a look over at the Layers panel and see which thumbnail is selected. Ninety percent of the time, that's the cause. Okay, now we can move on. See? I told you it was only a small lie.

COMBINING MULTIPLE IMAGES

LAYER MASKS LET YOU COMBINE MULTIPLE IMAGES WITHOUT ERASING PARTS OF THE IMAGE

If you think back to Chapter 1, we combined several images together in "Using Multiple Layers" by bringing them all into the same document and erasing parts of each layer away. That example was great for showing how layers work with each other and how you can see through part of one layer to the layer under it. However, when it comes to real life, it's not that easy. You change your mind, the client changes his mind, or something just changes about the project, and you realize that erasing away parts of a layer is a pain. Mainly because you can't bring those erased pixels back. You'd have to start all over again if you want to change something. Well, now we're going to take a look at doing the same thing with layer masks. Trust me, this stuff rocks! Once you see how easy it is, I promise you that you'll never go back to that Eraser tool again.

STEP 1: OPEN THE PHOTOS THAT YOU'D LIKE TO BLEND TOGETHER

For starters, open the photos that you'd like to blend together.

STEP 2: COPY-AND-PASTE ONE OF THE PHOTOS INTO THE BACKGROUND IMAGE

First, decide which image you want to use as your background. Click on one of the other photos, press Command-A (PC: Ctrl-A) to select the image, then press Command-C (PC: Ctrl-C) and Command-V (PC: Ctrl-V) to copy-and-paste it into the first image, so they're both in the same document. Here, I'll use the photo of the man running as the background and copy the city buildings into it. I'll position the city, using the Move tool (V), in the general area I want it to be in the collage. The top works well here. When you're done, you should have two layers in the same file.

STEP 3: ADD A LAYER MASK TO THE TOP LAYER

Click on the city buildings layer to select it. Then click on the Add Layer Mask icon at the bottom of the Layers panel to add a layer mask to it.

STEP 4: SELECT THE GRADIENT TOOL AND USE THE BLACK, WHITE GRADIENT

In this example, I'm going to blend the city buildings into the photo of the man running. If you recall, layer masks see only in black and white, and they don't care how you actually get black and white on them. So, let's try using a gradient to give a nice smooth blend. Select the Gradient tool from the Toolbox (or just press G). Then click on the gradient thumbnail in the top Options Bar, and choose the third gradient from the left in the Gradient Editor. It's the default Black, White gradient. Also make sure you click on the Linear Gradient (leftmost) icon in the Options Bar.

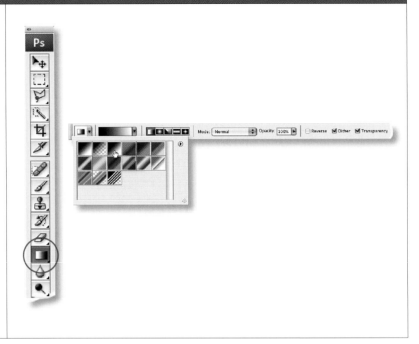

STEP 5: CLICK-AND-DRAG ON THE LAYER MASK TO BLEND THE CITY INTO THE PHOTO OF THE MAN

Now that you've got your gradient selected, we're going to use it on the layer mask. Click once on the layer mask on the city layer to make sure it's selected. Then click on the bottom of the buildings and drag upward. When you release your mouse button, you'll have created a gradient on the layer mask. More than that, though, look at your image. The city image blends nicely into the Background layer. If yours looks off, it's probably because of the way you dragged your gradient. Sometimes it takes a few tries, so feel free to drag over it again to adjust the gradient, as well as the overall blend.

STEP 6: BRING THE OTHER PHOTO INTO THE MAIN IMAGE

Now that we've got two photos in this collage, let's bring in the third. Copy-and-paste another photo into our main collage document that we've been working on. Use the Move tool to position it in the general area that you want it (at the bottom here). Now you should have three layers in the collage document. Go ahead and add a layer mask to this layer, as well, just like the other one.

STEP 7: SELECT THE BRUSH TOOL TO PAINT ON THE LAYER MASK

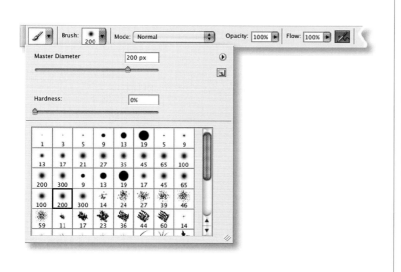

Now we need to blend the new layer into the image. We could use the Gradient tool again, but that's no fun. That's old news, right? Instead, let's try using the Brush tool because we can be a lot more precise in the areas we blend. Remember, we did this with our adjustment layer back in Chapter 3 when we had to hide the background around the couple from the Curves adjustment. So select the Brush tool (B). Click on the brush thumbnail in the Options Bar and set the diameter to something fairly large, like 200 pixels. Then set the Hardness to 0% so the edges are very soft and feathered.

STEP 8: PAINT WITH BLACK ON THE LAYER MASK

Now, click once on the layer mask thumbnail to select it. Press D, then X to set your Foreground color to black. Start painting on the area of the knife and fork that you want to hide (mainly over the man, so you can now see him running again). As you paint, that area of the photo will disappear.

STEP 9: IF YOU HIDE AN AREA THAT YOU DIDN'T WANT TO, PAINT IT WITH WHITE TO BRING IT BACK

Let's say, for example, you hide an area of your photo that you didn't want to. Just switch your Foreground color to white (press the X key) and paint over it again. Wherever you paint with white, you'll start to bring back the original photo. This means you can get very creative and experiment with different degrees of blending your photos with each other.

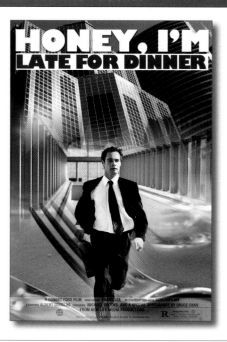

Lastly, I've added some movie elements to the design, since I always see this collaging effect used in movie posters.

A DEEPER LOOK INTO LAYER MASKS

LET'S TAKE A DEEPER LOOK INTO LAYER MASKS AND SOME OF THE COOL THINGS YOU CAN DO WITH THEM

Layer masks aren't just for collaging and blending photos, they're actually a very powerful selection and design tool. Let's take a look at a real project and see how layer masks can be used to make something appear in a photo that it didn't originally appear in. Plus, you'll see the effect of stacking multiple layers with layer masks on top of each other for an even better result.

STEP 1: OPEN THE IMAGES FOR THE MASKING PROJECT

Open the photos that you want to bring together with layer masks. In this example, I've got a photo of an LCD screen and a photo of a woman skiing. We'll use layer masks to make it appear as if she is breaking out of the LCD screen, and then put it onto the home-page of a website.

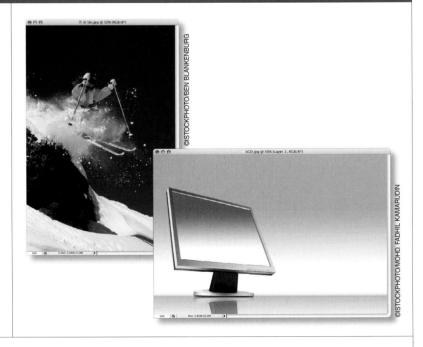

STEP 2: USE SELECT>COLOR RANGE TO SELECT THE SKIER FROM THE BACKGROUND

Start with the photo of the skier first. Click the Select menu and choose Color Range. Since we want to make it appear as if the skier is breaking out of something, we need to get rid of the sky. In the Color Range dialog, click on the photo near the top part of the sky. That tells Color Range to select those colors. With the preview set to Selection, you'll see the selected portion turn white. Press-and-hold the Shift key and click in other areas of the blue sky to select them, since the color gradates toward the bottom (Shift-click and select about five other points). Then, set the Fuzziness slider to 160 and click OK.

STEP 3: INVERSE THE SELECTION AND COPY IT TO ITS OWN LAYER

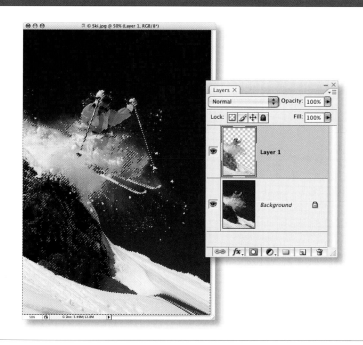

Right now, you should have the sky selected. What we really want is the skier selected, so click the Select menu and choose Inverse to reverse the selection (or press Command-Shift-I [PC: Ctrl-Shift-I]). Then, put this selection on its own layer by pressing Command-J (PC: Ctrl-J).

STEP 4: SELECT BOTH LAYERS AND MOVE THEM INTO THE LCD PHOTO. LINK THE TWO LAYERS

Select both layers in the Layers panel by Command-clicking (PC: Ctrl-clicking) on them. Then click-and-drag them over the LCD screen in that photo. Now you'll have three layers in the Layers panel, and the two skier layers should still be selected. Go ahead and click on the Link Layers icon on the far left at the bottom of the Layers panel to link these layers. Now, anytime you move one layer, the other will always follow. If they don't cover the screen completely, press Command-T (PC: Ctrl-T) to go into Free Transform, click the Link icon in the Options Bar, increase the Width percentage until they do, then press Return (PC: Enter) to lock it in.

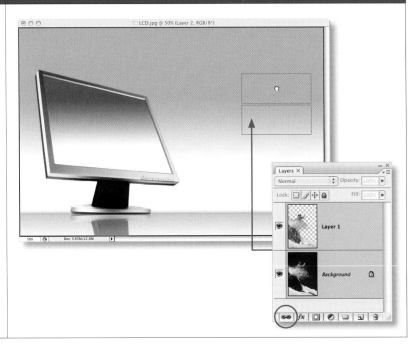

STEP 5: HIDE THE TWO SKIER LAYERS. USE THE POLYGONAL LASSO TOOL TO SELECT THE SCREEN

Click on the Eye icons in front of the two skier layers to hide them, so you can see the LCD again. Select the Polygonal Lasso tool from the Toolbox, or press Shift-L until you have it, and make a rectangular selection of the LCD screen.

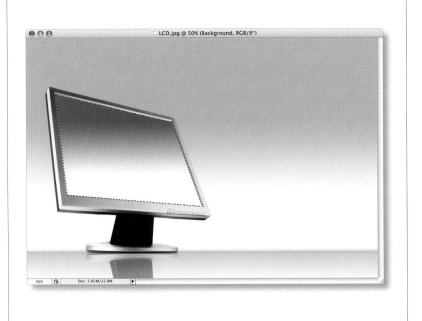

STEP 6: UNHIDE THE SKIER LAYERS AND ADD A LAYER MASK TO THE BOTTOM COPY

Click where those Eye icons used to be to unhide the two skier layers so you can see them again. Don't deselect yet, though. Click on the bottom skier layer (the entire photo), and click on the Add Layer Mask icon at the bottom of the Layers panel to add a layer mask to it. Photoshop automatically hides all parts of the layer that extend beyond the LCD screen. However, we still have the layer with only the skier on top of it, so we'll still see her.

STEP 7: COPY THE LAYER MASK BY OPTION-DRAGGING IT FROM ONE LAYER TO THE OTHER

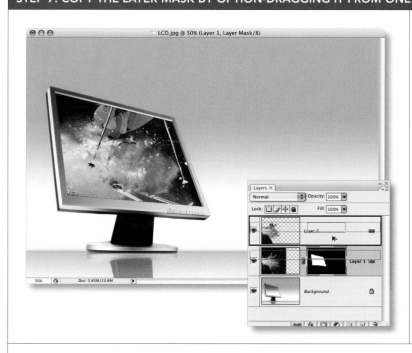

Now we'll want to apply that same layer mask to the layer above it. The last thing we want to do, though, is make the selection all over again. Instead, we'll just copy the layer mask. The easiest way to copy a layer mask is to press-and-hold the Option (PC: Alt) key and click-and-drag the layer mask from one layer to another. This duplicates the mask onto the other skier layer. Notice that it hides any areas that extend beyond the LCD screen, though, including part of her arms, head, and skis. No problem—we'll take care of that in a minute.

STEP 8: WHAT HAPPENS IF YOU NEED TO REPOSITION THE LAYERS?

Before we move on, I want to show you some tips you'll use often. See, back in Step 4 we moved the two layers of the skier on top of the LCD screen and just left them there. But what happens if you decide later you want to move them and you've already added masks (as in this case)? I'm glad you asked. First, we just added a mask over the skier so we can't see most of her anymore. But I want to reposition her skis so they break out over the monitor, which means I'll need to see the layer without the mask. Easy stuff. Just Shift-click on the layer mask thumbnail in the Layers panel to temporarily disable the mask.

STEP 9: UNLINK THE LAYER MASK FROM THE LAYER SO YOU CAN MOVE IT

Before you jump ahead and move the layer, we need to do one more thing. There's a little link icon between the layer thumbnail and the layer mask thumbnail. This means that if we move the layer, the layer mask will follow because they're linked. However, that's not what we want here. We just want to move the layer and leave the mask where it is, since the LCD screen position won't change. So, click the link icon to turn it off. Remember, though, we have two skier layers linked together here, so you'll need to turn the other layer mask link off, too. Now select the Move tool (V) and move both layers. The masks will stay put. Relink the layer masks to the layers, and click on the top layer's mask to turn it back on.

STEP 10: SELECT THE BRUSH TOOL AND PAINT THE HIDDEN PORTIONS OF THE SKIER BACK IN

Okay, take a breath for a minute. Look at the Layers panel—specifically the top layer. It's the one of the skier with the sky removed. We added a layer mask to it in Step 7 that hid any areas that extend beyond the LCD screen. Right now, the only part of this layer we see is where the mask is white, right? We need to see the parts of the skier that extend beyond the screen to get that breaking out effect. Select the Brush tool (B), make sure you're Foreground color is white, and paint to reveal only the skier as she breaks out of the screen. Use a fairly large brush (I used a 100-pixel brush here) and don't worry if you reveal any extra areas. We'll get rid of them next.

STEP 11: ZOOM IN AND USE SMALLER BRUSH SIZES TO MAKE IT LOOK MORE REALISTIC

If yours looks like mine at this point, then you probably revealed too many extraneous areas around the skier in the last step. That's totally fine and actually it's better that way because now you can use the Zoom tool (Z) to zoom in, press X to switch your Foreground color to black, and paint with a smaller brush to hide all of those little areas that just don't fit. In this example, I hid any snow areas that appeared over the monitor edges so only the skier and her skis show up outside the monitor, not any of the little pieces of snow. This part takes a little time, though, so be patient and make it look good.

STEP 12: USE THE DODGE TOOL TO LIGHTEN THE SNOWFLAKES

If your image still looks like mine, you've also probably got some little blue outlines around some of the snowflakes. This happened when we selected the skier from the sky and is pretty normal. You can always choose to hide them with the layer mask. If you want to leave them in, however, select the Dodge tool from the Toolbox (or just press O). Click on the layer's thumbnail instead of the mask, set the Range to Shadows in the Options Bar, and set your Foreground color to black. Then paint over the edges of the snowflakes to lighten the darker colors. This should help them blend in.

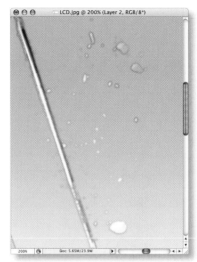

Before using the Dodge tool

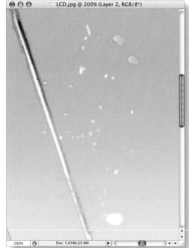

After using the Dodge tool

STEP 13: LET'S BRING IN A PHOTO FOR THE BACKGROUND

We're almost done. One thing we'll want to do is bring in a photo for the background of the webpage. So, open another photo. Select the Rectangular Marquee tool (M) and make a large rectangular selection. Then click the Select menu and choose Modify>Smooth. Enter 20 pixels for the Sample Radius, and click OK.

STEP 14: COPY-AND-PASTE THE BACKGROUND PHOTO INTO OUR WEBPAGE IMAGE. ADD A WHITE STROKE

Copy-and-paste the selection into our main webpage image by pressing Command-C (PC: Ctrl-C), switching to the webpage image, and pressing Command-V (PC: Ctrl-V). Choose Edit>Free Transform to resize it and position it toward the top middle of the image. Then Command-click (PC: Ctrl-click) on the layer thumbnail to put a selection around the photo. Click the Edit menu and choose Stroke. Enter 6 pixels for the Width and set the Color to white. Click OK, and now you'll have a white stroke around the selection. Press Command-D (PC: Ctrl-D) to Deselect.

STEP 15: MAKE A SELECTION AROUND THE ENTIRE LCD MONITOR

You'll notice that the large photo we just copied in covers the LCD and the skier. We've got to change that. So, guess what that means. Yep, another mask. This time, instead of selecting just the inside of the LCD screen, we've got to select the whole LCD monitor itself. Click on the Eye icon next to the snowy mountain photo layer to hide it. Grab the Polygonal Lasso tool again and make a selection around most of the monitor. It's okay if you don't select the bottom part, but make sure you get the whole screen and some of the stand. Once you've made the selection, unhide the layer.

STEP 16: ADD A LAYER MASK TO THE LARGE PHOTO LAYER AND INVERT IT

Since we have a selection active, go ahead and add a layer mask to the mountain photo layer. This masks the photo so it fits into the selection, which is actually the opposite of what we want. We want to see the photo everywhere but over the LCD. Well, that leads me to another cool tip—inverting. Click on the layer mask and choose Image>Adjustments>Invert. This inverts, or reverses, the color of everything on a layer. Black becomes white and white becomes black.

TIP: To avoid going to the Image menu for Invert all the time, just press Command-I (PC: Ctrl-I) instead.

Before Invert

After Invert

STEP 17: MOVE THE MOUNTAIN LAYER BELOW THE SKIER. BRING IN THE FINAL ELEMENTS

Now, click on the mountain photo layer and drag it below the skier layers so she doesn't cover the photo. Now add the final elements that make up the webpage. Here, they're pieces in another file, but you could just as easily create the text right here in the document itself (see Chapter 5 for more on creating text).

MAKING ONE LAYER FIT INTO ANOTHER

FORCING THE CONTENTS OF ONE LAYER TO FIT INSIDE THE CONTENTS OF ANOTHER LAYER

There's another masking feature that comes in really handy. It's called a clipping mask, and it's another type of mask that we use with layers. Its main purpose is letting you use a shape on one layer to mask layers above it. Clipping masks have a ton of good uses, but one great example is creating some type of card—be it a credit card, membership card, or gift card.

STEP 1: CREATE A NEW BLANK DOCUMENT

We'll kick this one off by creating a brand new blank document. Click on the File menu and choose New (or just press Command-N [PC: Ctrl-N]). In the New dialog, type the size of the final image you want to create. In this example, I'll create a document that is 800x600 pixels at a resolution of 72 ppi. Click OK to create the new document.

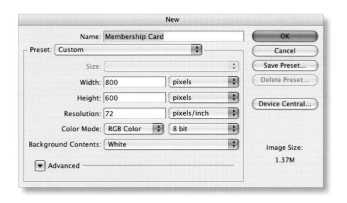

STEP 2: CREATE A ROUNDED RECTANGLE SELECTION FILLED WITH BLACK ON A NEW LAYER

Select the Rectangular Marquee tool (M). Create a rectangle in the middle of the canvas. Then click the Select menu and choose Modify>Smooth. Enter 15 pixels for the Sample Radius and click OK. This creates a rounded rectangular selection. Now click on the Create a New Layer icon at the bottom of the Layers panel to create a new blank layer. Press D to set your Foreground color to black, and press Option-Delete (PC: Alt-Backspace) to fill the selection with black. Press Command-D (PC: Ctrl-D) to Deselect.

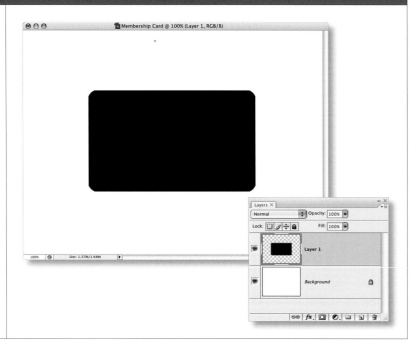

STEP 3: COPY-AND-PASTE THE PHOTO YOU WANT TO APPEAR ON THE CARD ONTO A NEW LAYER

Open the photo that you want to appear on the card. In this example, we're creating a membership card for an airline, so we'll use a photo of an airplane. Press Command-A (PC: Ctrl-A) to select the photo. Press Command-C (PC: Ctrl-C), then switch documents, and press Command-V (PC: Ctrl-V) to copy-and-paste the photo into the card image we just created. Make sure it's on a layer above the card layer in the Layers panel.

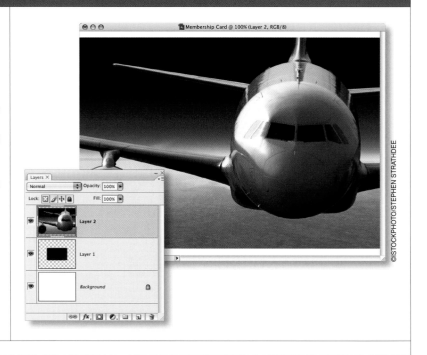

©ISTOCKPHOTO/STEPHEN STRATHDEE

STEP 4: CREATE A CLIPPING MASK TO FORCE THE AIRPLANE TO FIT INSIDE THE CARD

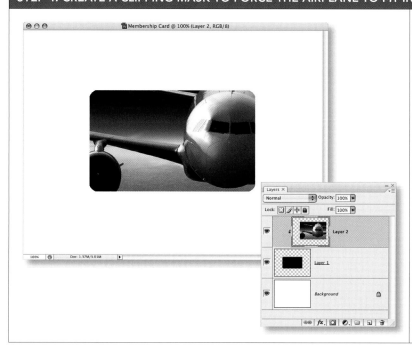

Click once on the airplane layer to select it. Click the Layer menu and choose Create Clipping Mask, or just press Command-Option-G (PC: Ctrl-Alt-G). This forces the photo of the airplane to only appear inside the boundaries of the layer below it. Even better, select the Move tool (V) and move the airplane photo around. You'll see that you can move it around anywhere you want and it still only reveals itself inside that original card shape. In fact, you can resize it, as well. Just choose Edit>Free Transform, or press Command-T (PC: Ctrl-T), and resize at will.

STEP 5: ADD A RECTANGULAR SELECTION FILLED WITH GRAY ON A NEW LAYER. REDUCE THE OPACITY

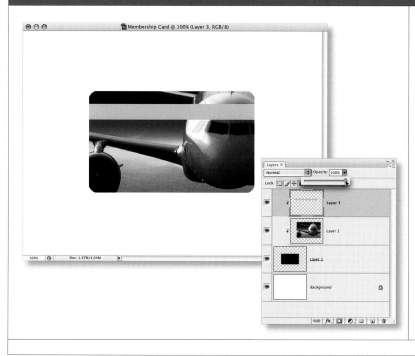

Create another new layer and use the Rectangular Marquee tool to make another rectangular selection. Don't worry about how wide the rectangle is at this point. Set your Foreground color to a light gray color (I used R: 205, G: 205, B: 205 here), and use the Paint Bucket tool (nested below the Gradient tool) to fill the selection by clicking on it. Choose Select> Deselect. Drop the opacity of the gray rectangle layer to 70%. You'll see the rectangle appears outside the boundaries of the card, though. Just click the Layer menu and choose Create Clipping Mask again, and the same thing that happened to the airplane photo will happen to the rectangle.

STEP 6: SO WHAT IS REALLY GOING ON HERE?

The natural question to follow all this cool stuff is what the heck is really going on here? Think of it this way: the bottom layer (or base layer) of a clipping mask is the shape you want to see in the final image. In this case, it's taken the form of a membership card, but it doesn't always have to be that way. It could be any shape—circle, square, logo, clip art, text, etc. That base layer tells Photoshop what shape or object you want to see in the end. Everything else that appears on top of that layer is what you'll actually see in the image.

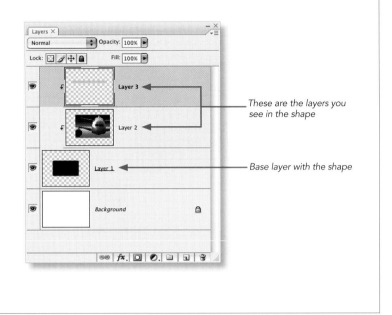

These are the layers you see in the shape

Base layer with the shape

STEP 7: ADD A HUE/SATURATION ADJUSTMENT LAYER. CLIP IT SO IT AFFECTS ONLY THE CARD SHAPE

Let's change the color of the airplane photo a little. Click on the Create New Adjustment Layer icon at the bottom of the Layers panel and add a Hue/Saturation adjustment layer. Turn on the Colorize checkbox, and drag the Hue slider to 207, Saturation to 55, and Lightness to –9. Click OK. See how the Hue/Saturation adjustment not only affects the airplane, but the entire white background? Go ahead and create a clipping mask of this layer, too. This allows you to use an adjustment layer to only affect the layer below it. One more thing: drag the Hue/Saturation adjustment layer below the gray rectangle layer to only apply the adjustment to the airplane photo.

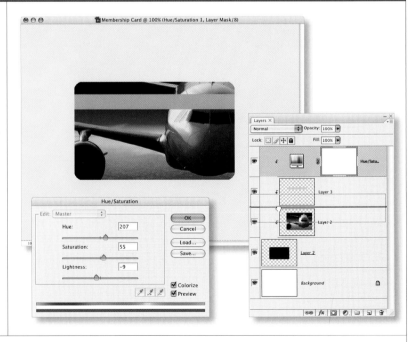

STEP 8: ADD SOME MORE RECTANGLE SHAPES ON THEIR OWN LAYERS AND CLIP THEM

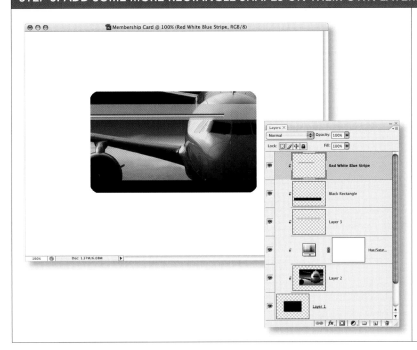

Add a few more blank layers and create some rectangular shapes on them. Then create clipping masks of all of them so they fit into the card. Here, I've added a black shape and positioned it at the bottom of the card. I've also added some red, white, and blue rectangles and put them over the light gray rectangle.

TIP: You don't have to keep going to the Layer menu to create a clipping mask. Just press-and-hold the Option (PC: Alt) key and position your cursor on the little divider line between two layers. You'll see two little circle icons appear. Click and that will automatically create a clipping mask of the layer on top.

STEP 9: ADD LOGOS, TEXT, AND GRAPHICS TO FINISH OFF THE CARD

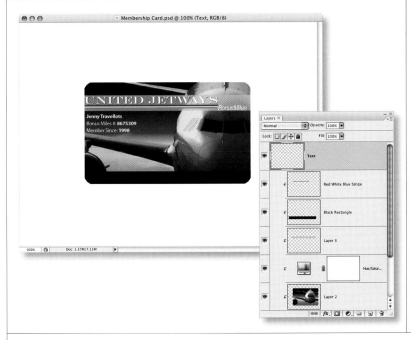

Add any logos, text, and graphics to the card. I had each of these in a separate file and just copied them into this document. Make sure you place them on layers above all of the other graphics. In fact, it's even better to place them in a group on top of everything else. There's no need to create clipping masks, though, because they don't extend beyond the boundaries of that original card shape.

STEP 10: DUPLICATE THE BLACK CARD LAYER TO CREATE A DROP SHADOW

If you want to really put the finishing touch on our membership card, then create a drop shadow below everything. Click on the black rounded rectangle layer that has served as the base layer here. Press Command-J (PC: Ctrl-J) to duplicate it.

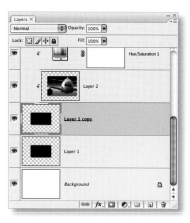

STEP 11: ADD A DROP SHADOW BY BLURRING THE LAYER AND REDUCING THE OPACITY

Click the bottom copy of the black rectangle layer in the Layers panel to select it. Then, click the Filter menu and choose Blur>Gaussian Blur. Set the Radius to 5 pixels and click OK. Finally, use the Move tool (V) to move the layer down and to the right a little and drop the layer's opacity to around 50%. Notice as you move this layer around, it doesn't affect the clipping masks above. That's because Photoshop is just looking at the one layer beneath all of the clipping mask layers and we haven't moved that one.

IDEA 1: HERE'S ANOTHER USE FOR CLIPPING MASKS: PUTTING A PHOTO INTO TEXT

Another really popular technique that clipping masks are used for is to make a photo appear inside of text. Just create a Type layer (more on that in Chapter 5) and move a photo onto a layer above it using the Move tool. Then click on the photo layer and create a clipping mask with it. Now you'll only see the photo inside of the shape of the text.

IDEA 2: CLIPPING MASKS ALSO COME IN HANDY FOR WEDDING ALBUM PAGE DESIGN

Clipping masks can also be used to place a photo into a shape. This works great when creating album page designs for weddings, family photos, or even senior portraits. You can use any of the selection or Shape tools (more about Shape tools in Chapter 5) to create a shape on a layer. Then put a photo on the layer above it. Add a clipping mask to that photo layer, and now it only appears inside of the shape. There are lots of possibilities here, but this wedding album page design is one.

HOW DO I...

? TURN OFF OR DISABLE A LAYER MASK?

Shift-click on the layer mask thumbnail in the Layers panel. You'll see a red X appear over it. It's still there, but the layer mask is disabled. Shift-click again on it to enable it.

? VIEW THE CONTENTS OF A LAYER MASK?

To see the contents of a layer mask, or see it in black-and-white mode, Option-click (PC: Alt-click) on it. Now you'll just see the mask onscreen, and you can adjust it (paint on it) there just as you normally would. Option-click on it again to get back to the normal view.

? MOVE A LAYER MASK TO ANOTHER LAYER?

To move a layer mask, just click-and-drag the layer mask to another layer.

? COPY A LAYER MASK TO ANOTHER LAYER?

To copy a layer mask, press-and-hold the Option (PC: Alt) key and click-and-drag the layer mask to another layer. You'll see a double-arrow cursor indicating that you're duplicating the mask and not just moving it.

? DELETE A LAYER MASK?

Drag the layer mask to the Trash icon at the bottom of the Layers panel.

? MOVE THE CONTENTS OF A LAYER WITHOUT MOVING THE LAYER MASK ITSELF?

To move what is actually on the layer around in your image, but leave the layer mask exactly where it is, you need to unlink the two. Click on the little chain-link icon between the layer thumbnail and the layer mask thumbnail to unlink them. Click that space again to re-link the two.

? APPLY A LAYER MASK PERMANENTLY TO A LAYER?

To apply a layer mask permanently to a layer, so it actually deletes the masked areas, Control-click (PC: Right-click) on the layer mask icon. Then choose Apply Layer Mask from the contextual menu that appears.

CHAPTER FIVE

TYPE AND SHAPE LAYERS

There are two more popular categories of layers that we haven't covered yet: type layers and shape layers. While you use two different tools to create these layers, they actually have a lot in common, which is why I'm covering them together. Plus, if you've followed everything so far, then type and shape layers are a breeze. That doesn't mean they're not powerful, though. There are a lot of things we can do with these layers that you simply can't do (or would have a heck of a hard time doing) without them.

CREATING TYPE LAYERS

TYPE LAYERS ARE HOW YOU GET TEXT INTO YOUR PHOTOSHOP DOCUMENTS. BUT THERE ARE LOTS OF EXTRAS, TOO

Creating text in Photoshop is simple enough. In fact, I probably wouldn't need to write much of a tutorial for that: select the Type tool, click on the canvas, then type away. There...we're done! But there's a ton of other features when it comes to building images with professional-looking text and that's what we're going to cover in this tutorial. So, here's the deal: this is a type chapter, but it's no fun to just create text for the heck of it, so I created a little project. It's a newsletter page for a finance column.

STEP 1: YOU HAVE A CHOICE TO MAKE

So, you have two options. (1) Start here and open the PSD file (that you downloaded from the book's website listed in the introduction) and start adding type. You'll see that all of the background elements are already in place. (2) Since this is a layers book, after all, I didn't want to leave you with no insight as to how I created these layers. If you're the curious or overly ambitious type (get it? Type. I don't get it either actually), then you can watch a video on the same website that'll show you how to create the background. It's up to you, but I'll say this: the video has one totally kick-butt tip for layers in it that you won't find in the book, so it's worth watching. Either way, make sure you start out with the image you see here as the first step.

©ISTOCKPHOTO/MURAT BAYSAN AND MATT KLOSKOWSKI

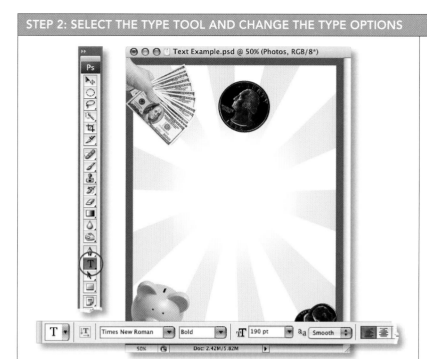

Select the Type tool (T) from the Toolbox. From the top Options Bar, select Times New Roman for the Font Family setting. Then choose Bold for the Font Style setting and enter 190 pt for the Font Size.

Next, click on the Foreground color swatch at the bottom of the Toolbox and, in the Color Picker, set your Foreground color to R: 64, G: 109, B: 18. Any text you create is automatically set to your Foreground color, so try to have that picked out ahead of time (you can change it later if you need to, though). Then click on the canvas and type the word *finance*. Click on the Move tool (V) in the Toolbox and then position the text in the top center of the image.

Select the Type tool again and click on the canvas to start typing the words *The Weekly*. Notice how the Type tool remembered your settings from the last time and created the same style of text? Same font. Same size. In fact, the text probably runs off the document.

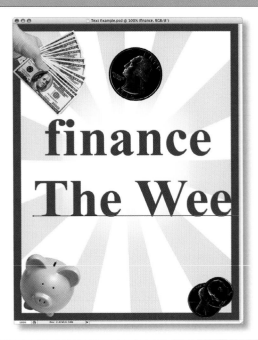

One of the cool features about type in Photoshop is that you're never stuck with it. You can always change your mind, and that's what we'll do for the text we just created. With The Weekly type layer selected in the Layers panel, go to the Options Bar and change the Font Family setting to something really thick—I used Rockwell Extra Bold here. Then change the Font Size to 40 pt, click on the Move tool in the Toolbox, and move the text above and just to the right of the letter *i* in the word *finance*.

Sometimes you'll want to edit text after you've already created it. Well that's the whole benefit of editable type—you can always change your mind. To edit your text, you've got two options: (1) double-click on the Type layer in the Layers panel to select the text and type something else, or (2) click on the text itself and drag over the specific letters you want to change to highlight them. Here, I've selected the word *Weekly* and changed it to *Daily*.

You're not stuck with the color of your text either. With The Daily text layer selected, click-and-drag over the word *The* to select it and then click on the Foreground color swatch in the Toolbox. In the Color Picker, change the color to black and click OK. Then select the word *Daily*, click on the Foreground color swatch again, change this text to a blue color (here I used R: 0, G: 75, B: 159), and then press Command-Return (PC: Ctrl-Enter) to commit the change.

Next, let's type the word *Journal* below the word *finance*. Just like before, it'll pick up the last font, size, and color you used, which is fine, but this time when you're done, select all of this new text. Then, click on the Font Family pop-up menu to show all of your fonts. You'll see a WYSIWYG (what-you-see-is-what-you-get) preview of each font installed on your computer on the right side of the menu so you can pick one visually.

The WYSIWYG preview is neat and all, but I have to be honest, it's not my preferred way of picking fonts. First, it's small. Second, it only shows the word *Sample*, which is fine if you type the word *Sample* all the time, but chances are you don't. Here's my preferred way: Select the text and click on the Font Family name in the pop-up menu in the Options Bar (it will become highlighted). Now, are you ready for this? Just press your Up or Down Arrow key to cycle through all of the fonts and Photoshop will automatically swap out the text on your canvas with the newly selected font. This way, you can get a live preview of the font you have selected.

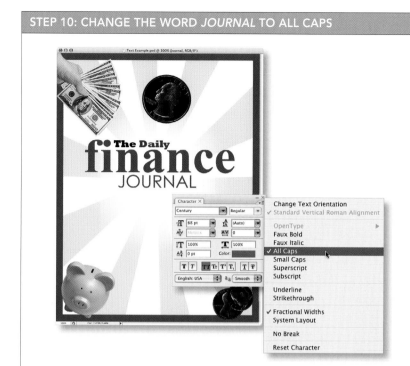

I've settled on the font Century Gothic for the Journal layer. I also changed the Font Size to 68 points and set the text color to the same green we used for the Finance layer. Now let's change the Journal layer to all caps. Instead of retyping, though, just click on the Window menu and choose Character. Then click on the arrow at the top right of the Character panel, and from the flyout menu, choose All Caps. It's just one word here so it would be no big deal to change it manually, but if you had more text it could be time consuming.

I'd also like to make the word *JOURNAL* appear as wide as the word *finance*. Now, I don't want to increase the font size, I just want to spread out the amount of space between each letter. We'll call on the Character panel for this since we just used it in Step 10. First, select the word *JOURNAL*, and then in the Character panel, go to the field with the little letters AV with a double-sided arrow under them. That's the Tracking setting. Click in the Tracking field and start hitting the Up Arrow key. You'll see the spacing between the letters start to increase. I set mine to 640 and used the Move tool (V) to position *JOURNAL* under *finance*.

The next thing we want to do is reduce the amount of space between some of the letters in the word *finance*. Take a look at the large amount of space between the first *n* and the *a*. The popular typography saying is: "You could drive a truck through that space." Seriously, though, see how some letters are further apart than others? This is a big no-no when it comes to making professional-looking type. This time, select the Finance layer and select just the two letters you want to bring closer together, then reduce the tracking instead of increasing it. Do this for any letters that seem too far apart from (or the opposite, too close to) each other.

Go ahead and add some more text to the page, following the example here. (For *manage your moola*, I used Monotype Corsiva set to 55 points in black, and I used Futura Medium Italic at 22 points for the small text at the bottom, also in black.) Then, go through and reduce the space between any letters that are too far apart in this text, just like we did in the previous step, as well as for the words *The Daily* at the top.

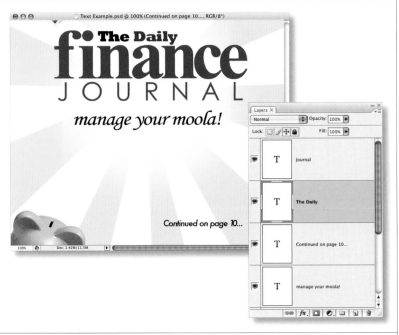

STEP 14: CREATE A LARGE BLOCK OF TEXT

The next thing I want to add is a large block of text. So far, all of the text we've created has been on one line. Now we want to add some text that spans multiple lines. You could just hit the Return (PC: Enter) key at the end of each line to go to the next one, but that's the hard way—it works, but it doesn't work well. Instead, we'll use a little trick with the Type tool to create a text block. First, select the Type tool (T) from the Toolbox, then click-and-drag to create a rectangle, just like you would with a selection tool. This creates a text box just waiting for you to type in it.

STEP 15: CHOOSE YOUR FONT AND START TYPING

Choose the font family, style, size, and color you want and start typing (I used Myriad Pro at 14 point in black). Watch what happens as you type near the end of the line, though. As your text hits the far-right side, it will automatically wrap to the next line. You don't have to do a thing. Of course, you could always manually hit the Return (PC: Enter) key if you wanted to put a hard line break in, but the whole point of using a text box is that you don't have to.

STEP 16: USE THE PARAGRAPH PANEL TO CHANGE ALIGNMENT AND/OR JUSTIFICATION

As soon as you create a text box, you open up a whole new set of possibilities for editing. Now you can use the Paragraph panel to change your type alignment and justification. Click on the Window menu and choose Paragraph. The alignment options are near the top left of the panel and the justification options are on the top right. For this example, click on the Justify Last Left icon (the fourth icon from the right) to make your text spread evenly across the entire text box.

STEP 17: TRY TO APPLY A GRADIENT OR FILTER TO A TYPE LAYER

We're almost done, but there are still a couple of things I'd like to do: First, I'd like to apply a gradient to the Finance layer, and I'd also like to apply a filter to it. Problem is, you really can't. Try it. Select the Finance layer in the Layers panel, and then select the Gradient tool (G) from the Toolbox. Position your cursor over your document and you'll see the little symbol for "no way." Also, try clicking on the Filter menu and choosing any filter. You'll get a dialog telling you your type needs to be rasterized first.

TIP: There are some workarounds for doing things like this on live Type layers. See Chapter 8, *Layer Styles*, and Chapter 9, *Smart Layers*, for more info.

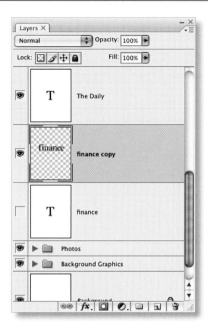

The point I'm trying to make is that your Type layers are special kinds of layers. There are certain things you can't do to them (like add filters or gradients or use a brush on them). To do these things, we need to rasterize the layer. It's easy to do, but the text will no longer be editable. Select the Finance layer and then press Command-J (PC: Ctrl-J) to duplicate it. Hide the original (so we have a backup) by clicking on the Eye icon to the left of the layer thumbnail. Control-click (PC: Right-click) on the duplicate and choose Rasterize Type. This turns the Type layer into a regular old layer. Now you can apply gradients and filters, but you can't change the text anymore, so there's a tradeoff.

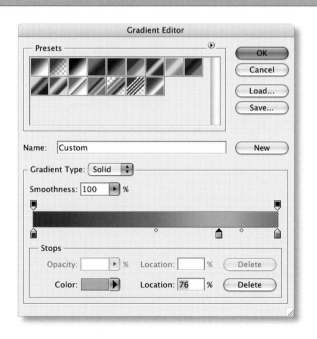

Select the Gradient tool again from the Toolbox and click on the gradient thumbnail in the Options Bar. This opens the Gradient Editor. Now let's create a gradient that starts on the left with a dark green, then goes to a lighter green, and ends up with a medium-dark green. First, double-click on the Color Stop on the bottom left of the Gradient Bar. From the Color Picker, choose a dark green (I chose R: 48, G: 92, B: 28). Add another Color Stop to the bottom right of the gradient ramp by clicking beneath it. Double-click on that new Color Stop and choose a lighter green (R: 157, G: 207, B: 37). Finally, double-click on the bottom-right Color Stop and choose a medium-dark green (R: 107, G: 160, B: 28).

In the Options Bar, click on the Linear Gradient icon (the first icon to the right of the gradient thumbnail). We'll click-and-drag the gradient from top to bottom on the word *finance*. However, there's one little trick: If we just click-and-drag on this layer, it'll fill the whole layer. So, click on the Lock Transparent Pixels icon at the top left of the Layers panel. This locks everything that is transparent. Now click-and-drag from the top of the word *finance* to the bottom to add the gradient.

Finally, let's apply a filter to the text. Again, you wouldn't have been able to do this before you rasterized the text back in Step 18. The last thing I want to do is give some texture to the *finance* text, so click on the Filter menu and choose Artistic>Underpainting. On the left side of the dialog, you can use the default settings: set the Brush Size to 6, Texture Coverage to 16, Texture to Canvas, Scaling to 100%, and Relief to 4. Click OK to apply the filter and you're done. At this point, you've seen just about everything there is with Type layers in Photoshop. So sit back and take a breather because Shape layers are cool, too, and that's what we're covering next.

ALL ABOUT SHAPE LAYERS

ADD A WHOLE NEW DIMENSION TO YOUR IMAGES WITH PHOTOSHOP'S SHAPE LAYERS

Photoshop's Shape layers are one of those overlooked areas that are really very powerful. What if you need to create a shape but you just can't do it with any of the selection tools? Shape tools can help. If you want to create a Web icon or button, then you'll love Shape layers. If you need to go beyond simple shapes and create your own complex ones, then Shape layers are the place to turn. You can even save them as a preset so you can use them again later. There are literally thousands of possibilities. If you've never given shapes in Photoshop the time of day, then check out this tutorial and learn how to start putting them to work for you.

STEP 1: CREATE A NEW BLANK DOCUMENT

Start out by creating a new blank document by choosing File>New. Enter 1024x768 pixels for the width and height and 72 ppi for the resolution. Name your new document and click OK.

New		
Name: Shape Layers		OK
Preset: Custom		Cancel
Size:		Save Preset...
Width: 1024	pixels	Delete Preset...
Height: 768	pixels	
Resolution: 72	pixels/inch	Device Central...
Color Mode: RGB Color	8 bit	
Background Contents: White		Image Size:
Advanced		2.25M

Now select the Rectangle tool (U) from the Toolbox. Notice that this isn't the Rectangular Marquee tool—it's the Rectangle tool and it's located further down in the Toolbox. If you click-and-hold on it in the Toolbox, you'll see a pop-up menu with a few other shapes, as well, but we just want the Rectangle tool for now. Take a look in the top left of the Options Bar and you will see there are three little icons. The first one is the Shape Layers icon, so make sure you click on it to select it. That ensures that we create a Shape layer.

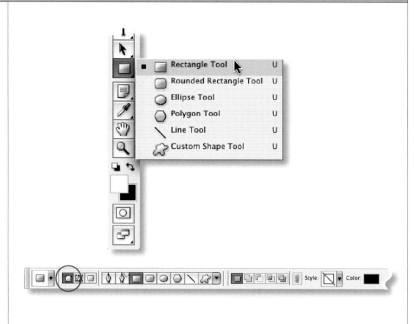

Press D to set your Foreground color to black and then click-and-drag out a rectangle across the bottom of the canvas with the Rectangle tool. If you don't position it correctly the first time, just press-and-hold the Spacebar to move it around as you click-and-drag.

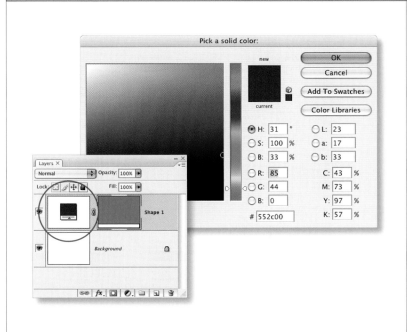

After you create the shape, you'll notice a new layer appear in the Layers panel. This layer should look pretty different from anything that we've seen before this chapter—it's a Shape layer. Shape layers are cool for a few reasons—one of them being, you can change its color by simply double-clicking on the layer thumbnail (the one on the left of the layer). Try it: double-click on the Shape layer thumbnail and in the resulting Color Picker, change the color to R: 85, G: 44, B: 0.

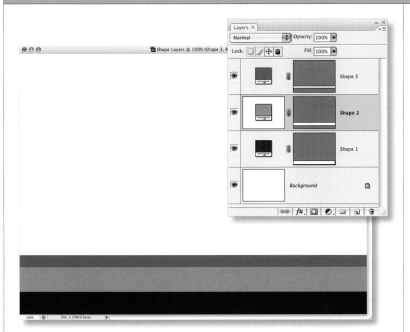

Create two more rectangle Shape layers. Make one the color R: 238, G: 152, B: 3, and the other one R: 0, G: 152, B: 202. Use the Move tool (V) to position these layers so they appear more toward the bottom of the image. Keep in mind that in order to see these Shape layers, they'll need to be above the first one we created in the Layers panel.

STEP 6: CREATE ANOTHER RECTANGLE SHAPE AT THE TOP OF THE IMAGE

In the Layers panel, select the Shape 1 layer and press Command-J (PC: Ctrl-J) to duplicate this layer. This will create another rectangle the same dark brown as the original rectangle that we drew on the bottom in Step 3. In the Layers panel, move this layer to the top of the layer stack. Then, in the document, with the Move tool (V), move the duplicate rectangle (which is currently at the bottom of the document on top of your original) to the top of the image.

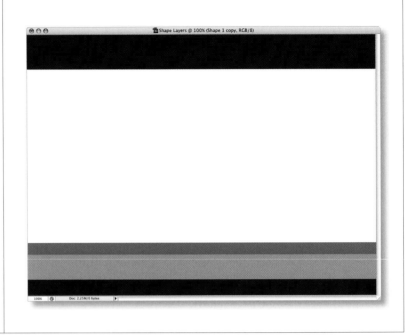

STEP 7: SELECT THE ELLIPSE TOOL AND ADD TO THE RECTANGLE SHAPE WE JUST CREATED

Another cool feature of Shape layers is that you're not stuck with the shape once you draw it. There are lots of ways to change them. You can always choose Edit>Free Transform. However, there's something even better: Select the Ellipse tool (press Shift-U until you have it) this time and press-and-hold the Shift key. You'll see a little plus sign icon at the bottom right of your cursor. Click-and-drag a circle that intersects with the bottom of the rectangle at the top of the image (press-and-hold the Spacebar while clicking-and-dragging to move the circle as you create it). Take a look over at the Shape 1 copy layer in the Layers panel. You've just added to that shape without creating another Shape layer.

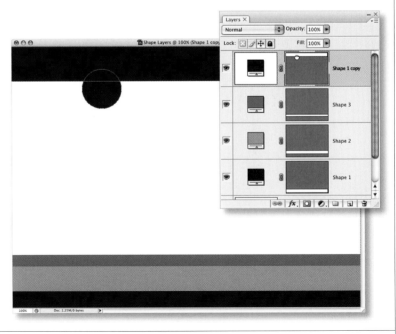

CHAPTER 5 | TYPE AND SHAPE LAYERS

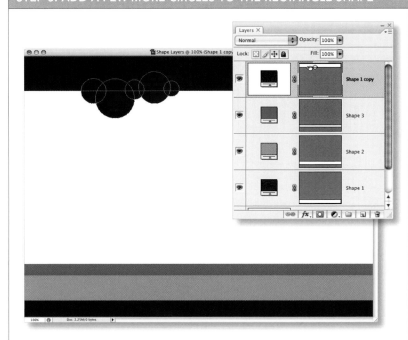

Keep pressing-and-holding the Shift key and click-and-drag a few more circles to give the appearance of a puffy cloud in the sky. Notice they all appear on the Shape 1 copy layer.

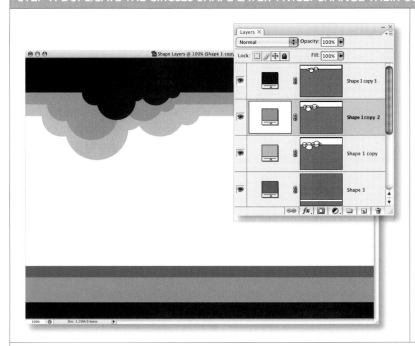

Press Command-J (PC: Ctrl-J) twice to duplicate the Shape 1 copy layer so there are three total. Change the color of the first duplicate layer (Shape 1 copy 2) to R: 238, G: 152, B: 3, and the color of the original circles layer (Shape 1 copy) to R: 243, G: 193, B: 0. With this bottom circles layer still selected, choose Edit>Free Transform. Grab one of the corner points and click-and-drag to make this layer larger. Another cool feature of Shape layers is that you can resize them without losing quality. Just make this Shape layer larger and it's still as crisp as it was when we created it. Do the same for the first duplicate layer, so now you have three on top of each other, but all different sizes.

You've now seen how to add to a Shape layer, but you can also subtract from it, as well. First, click on the blue Shape layer in the Layers panel (the one near the bottom of the image) to select that layer. One thing to watch out for is that even though you've selected that layer, you may not have selected the shape itself for editing. To do that, you've got to click on the gray thumbnail (it's called a vector mask) on the right side of the layer (to the right of the Shape layer thumbnail). You'll know you've selected it when you see an outline around the thumbnail as well as around the shape on your canvas.

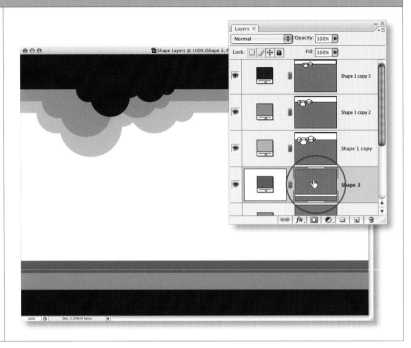

Once you've got the blue Shape layer selected, get the Ellipse tool again. This time press-and-hold the Option (PC: Alt) key and click-and-drag a small circle that intersects with the top portion of the rectangle and goes down to the bottom (just press-and-hold the Spacebar to move it around as you click-and-drag). Release your mouse button and you'll see that the area where the two shapes intersected is removed from the overall shape you see onscreen. Look over at the Layers panel and your Shape layer now looks different.

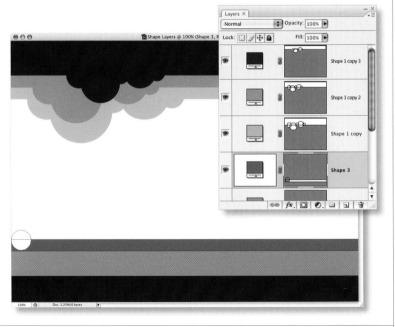

STEP 12: SUBTRACT SMALL CIRCLES ALL THE WAY ACROSS THE BLUE SHAPE LAYER TO MAKE WATER

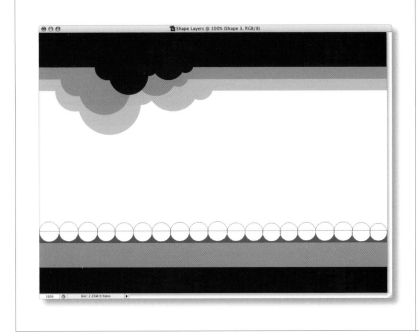

Do this multiple times to subtract small circles along the top of the blue rectangle shape to simulate waves in the water. To create circles that are just about the same size, click-and-drag a new circle over the previous one. Then press-and-hold the Spacebar to move it over to the next position in the rectangle and release your mouse button.

STEP 13: USE THE CUSTOM SHAPE TOOL TO ADD SOME BIRDS

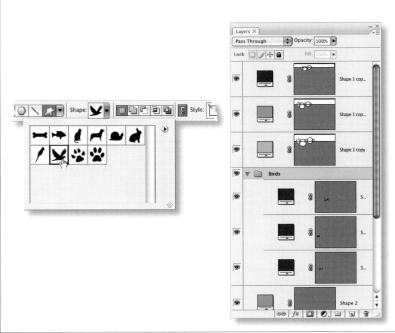

The Custom Shape tool is another tool in the same group as the Rectangle and Ellipse tools. After you select it (press Shift-U until you have it), click on the down-facing arrow next to the word *Shape* in the Options Bar to open the Shape Picker. Then click on the right-facing arrow in the Shape Picker, and from the flyout menu, load the animal shapes by choosing Animal. Click on the flying bird shape in the Shape Picker and then click-and-drag to create a few birds, and make them the darker brown color we've been using (see Step 4). To help keep things organized in the Layers panel, it's a good idea to put all the bird layers into a group by selecting them all in the Layers panel and then pressing Command-G (PC: Ctrl-G).

So far, we've been using shapes that Photoshop comes with. You can also make and use your own. Open the image of this black palm tree. Select the Magic Wand tool from the Toolbox (press Shift-W until you have it) and click on the black palm tree to select it (Shift-click on any missed areas to add to the selection). Before we can turn this into a custom shape, we need to turn it into a path first. Click the Window menu and choose Paths to open the Paths panel. Then click the Make Work Path from Selection icon at the bottom of the Paths panel. This turns the selection into a path, which is the first step in making a custom shape.

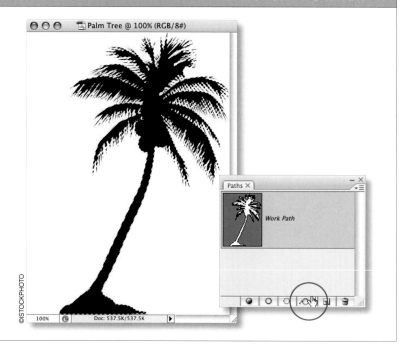

Now that you have a path created, click the Edit menu and choose Define Custom Shape. Give it a descriptive name in the Shape Name dialog, like Palm Tree, and click OK. Now you've got a custom shape ready to use in any image, not just this one.

STEP 16: USE YOUR NEW CUSTOM SHAPE TO ADD A PALM TREE TO THE SCENE

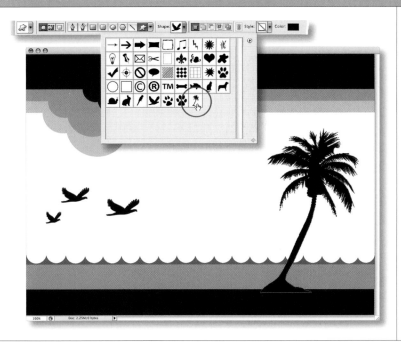

Go back to the sunset image we've been working on. Select the Custom Shape tool again. This time, from the Shape Picker in the Options Bar, choose the Palm Tree shape you just created. Click on the Foreground color swatch at the bottom of the Toolbox and set your Foreground color to the same dark brown color we've been using (R: 85, G: 44, B: 0) and click-and-drag a palm tree shape in your image. Make sure it's positioned above the rectangle layers at the bottom of the image in the Layers panel. You don't want the water to appear on top of the palm tree.

STEP 17: ADD A FEW MORE PALM TREES, AS WELL AS A SUN

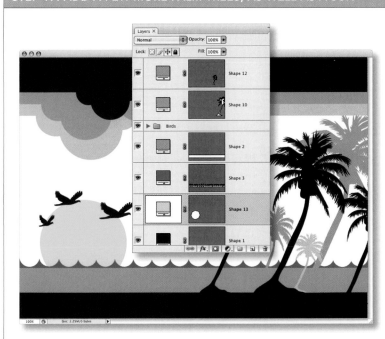

Add a few more palm trees to the image. Feel free to vary the size and the color of the trees to get some interesting effects. Use the Ellipse tool for one of the finishing touches and add a yellow circle (R: 255, G: 228, B: 0) for the sun. Position it so it looks like part of it is behind the waves by placing its layer near the bottom of the layer stack in the Layers panel. Your Layers panel is probably getting pretty unwieldy at this point, so make sure your sun appears behind the birds and make sure your trees don't fall behind the water.

STEP 18: ADD SOME TEXT TO THE TOP

Choose the Type tool (T) from the Toolbox and add some text along the top to cap things off. Here, I added a Type layer to the top of the Layers panel, used Bauhaus 93 for the font, and set the size to 110 pt. I also changed the color to R: 238, G: 152, B: 3.

STEP 19: MAKE THE IMAGE AS LARGE AS YOU WANT AND WATCH HOW IT DOESN'T LOSE ANY QUALITY

The last thing left to do is really just a quick demonstration to show you one last really cool feature of Shape layers (and Type layers for that matter). Click the Image menu and choose Image Size. Change the size to something really big—triple what the size is now—then click OK. If you look at the newly sized image at 100%, you'll see the edges are still perfectly crisp and no quality was lost on any Shape or Type layer. That's because Shape and Type layers are vector layers. That's just a techie way of saying they aren't pixels. You can always resize them without losing any quality.

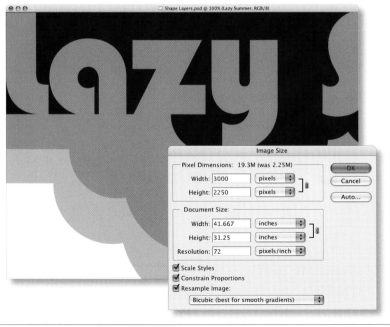

HOW DO I...

? QUICKLY SELECT MY TEXT?

Double-click on the Type layer thumbnail (the thing with the T on it) in the Layers panel. That selects all of the type on that Type layer.

? QUICKLY SEE WHAT DIFFERENT FONT FAMILIES WILL LOOK LIKE ON MY TEXT?

First, double-click the Type layer to select your text. Then click once in the Font Family pop-up menu. Use your Up and Down Arrow key to cycle up or down your font list and preview onscreen what a different font will look like. If you don't like any of them, just press the Esc key.

? HIDE THE HIGHLIGHT AROUND MY TEXT WHEN I'M TRYING TO SEE WHAT A DIFFERENT FONT LOOKS LIKE?

Press Command-H (PC: Ctrl-H). Make sure you remember you did it, though, and press it again to see the highlight later.

? CHANGE THE SIZE OF THE FONT SAMPLE PREVIEW IN THE FONT FAMILY POP-UP MENU?

Yep, that little font preview that says *Sample* is resizable. If you want to make it larger, go to Photoshop's preferences (Photoshop>Preferences on a Mac or Edit>Preferences on a PC). Then choose Type on the left-hand side to go to Type Preferences. Change the Font Preview Size setting to something larger and click OK.

? MAKE MY FONT SIZE LARGER OR SMALLER WITHOUT GOING TO THE FONT SIZE SETTING IN THE OPTIONS BAR?

Press Command-Shift-> (PC: Ctrl-Shift->) to make your font size larger or press Command-Shift-< (PC: Ctrl-Shift-<) to make it smaller.

? DUPLICATE A TYPE LAYER?

Press Command-J (PC: Ctrl-J), just like you would any other layer.

? OPEN THE CHARACTER PANEL?

The long way is to click the Window menu and choose Character. The quick way is to press Command-T (PC: Ctrl-T). You've got to have some text selected first, though, to use the shortcut. Otherwise that shortcut will take you into Free Transform mode.

? OPEN THE PARAGRAPH PANEL?

Choose Window>Paragraph.

CHAPTER SIX

ENHANCING PHOTOS WITH LAYERS

This chapter is all about enhancing digital photography. It's about making the photos that you see on your computer (and eventually print out) look like they did when you were there taking the photo. Throughout this chapter, I think you'll see one common theme (yes, besides techniques to enhance your photography), and that is simplicity. These techniques don't take 50 layers to achieve. In fact, you won't win any prizes for using a bunch of layers to enhance your photos. For me, it's quite the opposite. The fewer layers I use, the easier it is to work, and the more I get done.

COMBINING MULTIPLE EXPOSURES

ONE OF THE HOTTEST THINGS TO DO RIGHT NOW IN PHOTOGRAPHY IS TO COMBINE TWO EXPOSURES INTO ONE

If you've ever taken a photo only to find the sky is totally blown out but the rest of the photo looks fine, then this tutorial is for you. Here's why: When you take a photo that has a bright sky in it, you have to make a choice. Do you want to set your camera to expose for the sky so the sky looks good, or do you want to set it to expose for the foreground area or subject so that looks good? Many times, choosing one will make the other look bad. If you expose for the sky, then the foreground is typically very dark. If you expose for the foreground, then the sky will probably be too bright and lose all of the detail. Well, with a little planning ahead there's a workaround: multiple exposures. You can take one photo to expose for the sky and another one to expose for the foreground. Then, with layers and layer masks, there's a simple way to combine both and get the best of both worlds.

STEP 1: OPEN THE TWO PHOTOS THAT YOU'D LIKE TO COMBINE

Start out by opening the two photos that you'd like to combine. In this example, I took two photos of the same scene. First off, this depends heavily on shooting on a tripod, since you're going to over-lay these two photos and they need to match up. Next, I took the first photo with the purpose of making sure the sky looked good. As you can see, it does, but the foreground is way too dark. So, I left the tripod right where it was and took another photo and changed the exposure to make sure the foreground looked good. In doing that, you can see the sky is pretty blown out and lacking any detail.

STEP 2: BRING THE PHOTO WITH THE BAD SKY INTO THE PHOTO OF THE GOOD SKY

Copy-and-paste the photo that has the bad, blown-out sky into the other photo (the one with the good sky) by first clicking on the bad sky photo and pressing Command-A (PC: Ctrl-A) to select the entire image. Press Command-C (PC: Ctrl-C) to copy it, then click on the image with the good sky and press Command-V (PC: Ctrl-V) to paste the other photo into it. Now you should have both exposures in the same document, and it should have two layers in it. However, all you should see on the canvas is the photo that has the bad, bright sky.

STEP 3: ADD A LAYER MASK TO THE TOP LAYER

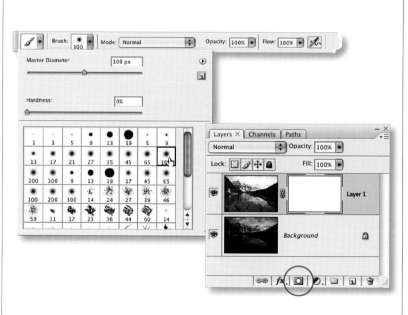

Click once on the top layer to make sure it is selected, and click on the Add Layer Mask icon at the bottom of the Layers panel to add a layer mask to it. Since there's an uneven area between the sky and the mountains, it's best we use a brush to blend the two photos together. So, select the Brush tool (B), click on the brush thumbnail in the Options Bar to get the Brush Picker, and choose a fairly large, soft-edged brush.

STEP 4: PAINT ON THE FOREGROUND AREA TO REVEAL THE PROPERLY EXPOSED SKY BELOW

Press D, then X to set your Foreground color to black and start painting on the sky to reveal the properly exposed sky from the layer below. You can even paint into the mountain area, because they look better on the bottom photo, too. To start off with, just paint the larger areas with the larger brush so you don't have to get too detailed.

STEP 5: DROP YOUR BRUSH SIZE AND ZOOM IN TO PAINT ALONG THE EDGE OF THE SKY

Now that you've got most of the layer below showing through, it's time to get a little more detailed. Drop your brush size to something really small. Then zoom in on the area where the sky meets the mountain. Use the smaller brush to paint along the edge of the sky and the mountain and trees. This part takes a little time because you really need to be precise here. The smaller the brush, the more precise you can be, but the longer it'll take.

TIP: Use the Left Bracket ([) key to quickly make your brush smaller.

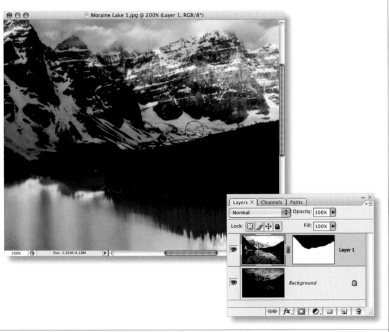

Inevitably, you'll paint too far into the mountains at some point and start to reveal the darker foreground from the layer below. If that happens, don't forget that you can switch your Foreground color to white and paint back any parts of the photo on the top layer.

TIP: Press the X key to swap your Foreground and Background colors. For example, if white is the Foreground color and black is the Background color, pressing X will swap them so black will be the Foreground color and white will then be the Background color.

PAINTING WITH LIGHT

THIS IS ONE OF THE HOTTEST WAYS TO IMPROVE YOUR PHOTOS AND REALLY DRAW ATTENTION TO THE SUBJECT

Every time I teach this technique, I get folks that ask me to do more. Here's why it's so cool, though. There really isn't more. What you see is what you get. It's simple, effective, and to the point. That's why I use it so much. One extra layer and I'm done. I think you'll agree—simple is better.

STEP 1: OPEN A PHOTO WHERE THE SUBJECT NEEDS MORE FOCUS

Start out by opening a photo where the subject needs more focus. Here, the bride's face is too dark and she blends into the background too much.

©ISTOCKPHOTO

STEP 2: ADD A CURVES ADJUSTMENT LAYER, THEN HIDE IT BY FILLING IT WITH BLACK

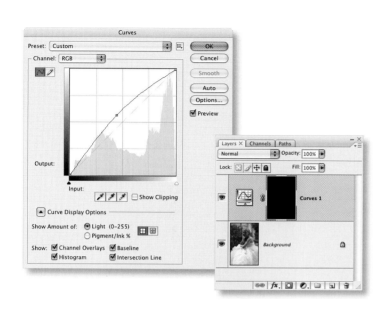

Now, go over to the Layers panel and click on the Create New Adjustment Layer icon at the bottom. Choose Curves to open the Curves dialog. Click on the middle of the curve to add a point, and drag it upward to lighten the entire photo. Don't go too crazy at this point. You can always come back later and tweak it if you need to. Click OK when you're done to add the adjustment layer. One more thing: Press Command-I (PC: Ctrl-I) to invert the white layer mask and turn it to black to hide the Curves adjustment for now.

STEP 3: PAINT WITH A LOW-OPACITY, WHITE BRUSH OVER KEY PARTS OF THE PHOTO

Select the Brush tool from the Toolbox, or just press B. Choose a medium-sized, soft-edged brush from the Brush Picker. Then set the brush's Opacity to 30% in the Options Bar. Press D to set your Foreground color to white (the default Foreground and Background colors are reversed on an adjustment layer) and start painting on the areas you want to add some extra light to. See? The painting with light title starts to make sense now, right?

STEP 4: BUILD THE LIGHTING EFFECT BY PAINTING MULTIPLE BRUSH STROKES

In the previous step, we set the brush opacity to 30%. That's because you want to be subtle here. You don't want your photo to look like it was lit in a fake way. If you need to add more light to specific areas, then just paint a stroke, release your mouse button, and click to paint again over it. You'll build the effect and make those brush strokes heavier each time, which, in turn, will add more light to the areas you brush over. Just make sure to reset the opacity when you're done. Also, if you want to see your mask to see how you're doing, then Option-click (PC: Alt-click) on it. You'll see the black-and-white version. Just Option-click again to see your image again.

STEP 5: TWEAK THE CURVES ADJUSTMENT LAYER TO ADD MORE OR LESS LIGHT

What's really cool about this lighting effect is that you can adjust it after the fact. Just double-click the Curves adjustment layer thumbnail in the Layers panel to open the Curves dialog again. Then click-and-drag the curve upward for more light or downward for less light. All that and it just took one layer. You gotta love this stuff!

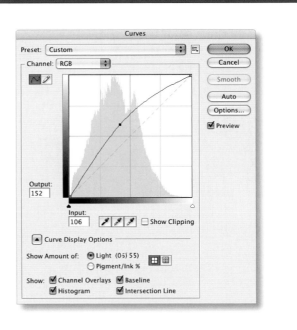

SELECTIVE SHARPENING

USE LAYERS TO SHARPEN ONLY SPECIFIC PARTS OF THE PHOTO THAT NEED IT MOST

Let's face it, sharpening isn't rocket science. It's actually very simple, so I don't want to complicate it with a bunch of layers and techie terminology. For me, the simplest form of sharpening usually looks the best. However, not all areas of a photo need to be (or should be) sharpened. Sometimes there are very specific parts that look good when sharpened, which is where this technique comes in. With one layer and a layer mask, we can get a tremendous amount of control in our sharpening.

STEP 1: OPEN A PHOTO THAT NEEDS TO BE SHARPENED

Start off by opening the photo that needs to be sharpened. Here, I'm taking one of those opportunities to show off one of my sons again. Hey, what can I say? I'm a dad, and I write books. You'd do the same if it were you, right? Plus, it's not like I'm flashing photos of my Aunt Ginny or Uncle Tony here (sorry Aunt Ginny and Uncle Tony). Anyway, here's a photo of Justin, and this technique is something I actually did to his photo before I printed it.

STEP 2: DUPLICATE THE LAYER AND APPLY THE SMART SHARPEN FILTER

Duplicate the Background layer so you have two copies of the image in the Layers panel. Then click the Filter menu and choose Sharpen>Smart Sharpen. This is a low-resolution photo, so I'm going to set the Amount to 50% and the Radius to 1 pixel. If it were a higher-resolution photo (150 ppi or higher), I'd use 75%–85% for the Amount. As far as the Remove setting, I always set it to Lens Blur and turn on the More Accurate checkbox because it does a better job of sharpening. Click OK when you're done to apply the sharpening.

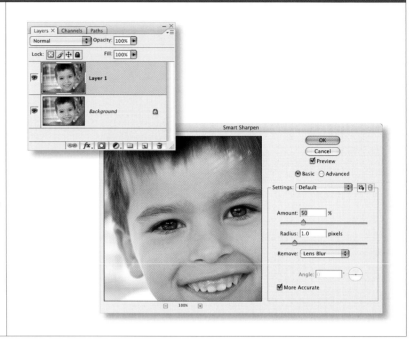

STEP 3: DUPLICATE THE SHARPENED LAYER AND APPLY EVEN MORE SHARPENING

Okay, that was just the first pass of sharpening to sharpen the overall photo. Now I want to take that sharpening a bit further to really make the eyes stand out, but I don't want to sharpen everything else again. Here's what to do: Duplicate the sharpened layer, so now there are three layers in the Layers panel. Go to the Smart Sharpen filter again and set the Amount to 50% again. Click OK, and you'll have sharpened the photo too much. In my example, his skin is starting to get a little bit of texture on it, which is a dead giveaway of too much sharpening. No problem, we'll take care of that in the next step.

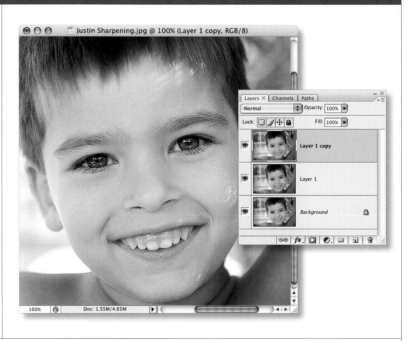

STEP 4: ADD A LAYER MASK TO THE SUPER-SHARPENED LAYER AND FILL IT WITH BLACK

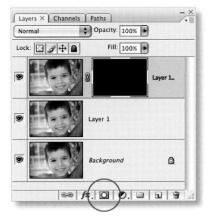

Click on the Add Layer Mask icon at the bottom of the Layers panel to add a layer mask to the top layer (the one we just over-sharpened). Then press Command-I (PC: Ctrl-I) to invert the white mask and fill it with black instead of white. This hides all of the sharpening effects on the twice-sharpened layer and reveals the once-sharpened layer beneath.

TIP: I use this one all the time, so read it! Press-and-hold the Option (PC: Alt) key when clicking the Add Layer Mask icon to automatically turn the mask black instead of white.

STEP 5: PAINT WITH WHITE TO REVEAL THE AREAS THAT NEED SOME TARGETED SHARPENING

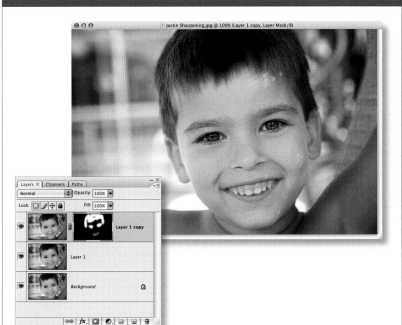

Get the Brush tool (B) and choose a small, soft-edged brush from the Brush Picker. Make sure your Foreground color is white, and start painting on the mask over the areas in the photo that can use some targeted sharpening. In this example, I've painted on his eyes, to really bring them out, his hair, and lightly on his mouth. What's great about this technique is that if it doesn't look good, you can just press X to swap your Foreground and Background colors and paint with black to hide the targeted sharpening. Either way, you have a huge amount of control here when it comes to sharpening your photos. At what cost, you ask? Just two layers.

DODGING AND BURNING DONE RIGHT

DODGING AND BURNING ARE TRADITIONAL TECHNIQUES THAT CAN STILL BE PUT TO EXCELLENT USE TODAY

Dodging and burning have their roots in the film days, and involve the selective lightening and darkening of parts of a photo. Because of that, there happen to be Dodge and Burn tools in Photoshop, but their effect is very much a permanent and destructive one. That said, I love using the concept of dodging and burning to really lead a person through the photo by lightening the areas I want them to focus on and darkening the parts of the photo that I don't. That's where this technique comes in, because it gives you all the flexibility of working with dodge and burn layers without any of the permanent effects.

STEP 1: OPEN A PHOTO THAT NEEDS SOME DODGING AND BURNING

Open a photo that looks kind of blah. I know, what kind of photo is blah, anyway? You'll know it when you see it. It's a photo that is worth keeping, but it just lacks that punch to take it to the next level. In the photo I'm using here, everything seems to blend together. Nothing really stands out. It's kind of, well, blah.

MATT KLOSKOWSKI

STEP 2: ADD A NEW LAYER AND FILL IT WITH 50% GRAY

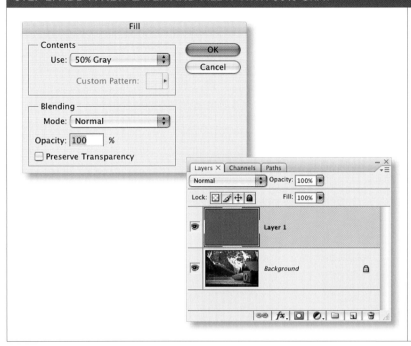

Click on the Create a New Layer icon at the bottom of the Layers panel to add a new, blank layer on top of the Background layer. Then, click the Edit menu and choose Fill. For the Use setting, select 50% Gray from the pop-up menu, and click OK.

STEP 3: CHANGE THE BLEND MODE TO OVERLAY. NOTICE HOW THIS MAKES THE GRAY TRANSPARENT

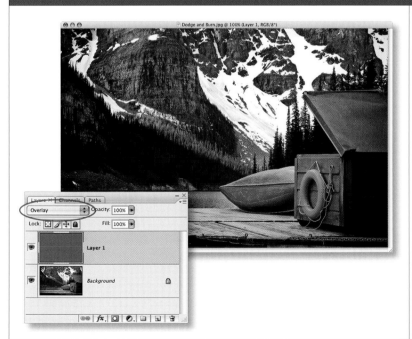

Change the blend mode of the gray layer you just made to Overlay. The Overlay blend mode hides everything that is 50% gray. This makes it appear that the gray layer is actually transparent. Go ahead, try clicking on the Eye icon next to the layer thumbnail to hide and show the layer. The image looks the same whether it's hidden or not.

TIP: You can also press Command-Shift-N (PC: Ctrl-Shift-N) to create the new layer and open the New Layer dialog. There you can change the blend mode to Overlay and fill with 50% gray, all in one shot.

STEP 4: SELECT THE BRUSH TOOL AND SET THE OPACITY OF THE BRUSH TO 20%

Now select the Brush tool (B) from the Toolbox. Choose a medium-sized, soft-edged brush—one that is large enough to paint inside most areas that you want to dodge and burn, but not too large that you'll be painting everything. Then set the Opacity setting of the brush to 20% in the Options Bar.

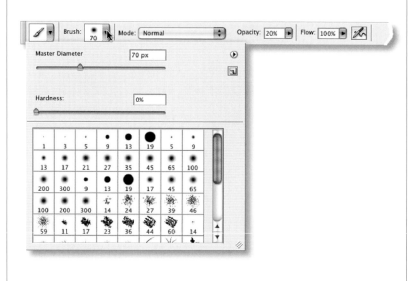

STEP 5: PAINT WITH WHITE TO SIMULATE DODGING

Click once on the gray layer to select it. Set your Foreground color to white by pressing D (for Default), then X (to swap). Now, start painting on areas in the photo that you want to dodge, or lighten. Since you're painting with a low-opacity brush, you can release the mouse button and click again to simulate multiple strokes of a brush. That'll intensify the effect and lighten the area even more. Look for key areas in the photo that you want to stand out. In this example, I'm painting over the canoe, the trees in the middle part of the photo, and even a little on the storage container and life preserver on its side.

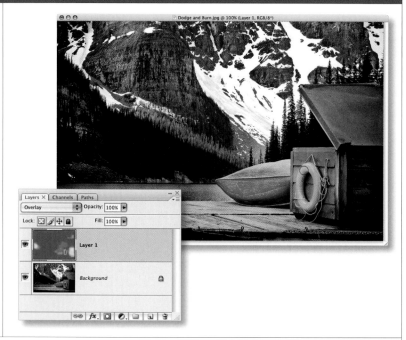

STEP 6: PAINT WITH BLACK TO SIMULATE BURNING

Now press X (to swap your Foreground and Background colors) to set black as the Foreground color. Paint in the areas that you want to burn, or darken. This is good around areas that you don't really want to draw people's attention to. In this case, I burned in some of the area on the mountains, and even the deck that the canoe is on. Don't forget to make your brush smaller so you can paint those smaller, more detailed areas.

TIP: Use the Left Bracket ([) key to quickly make your brush smaller.

STEP 7: PAINT WITH 50% GRAY TO GET BACK TO YOUR ORIGINAL

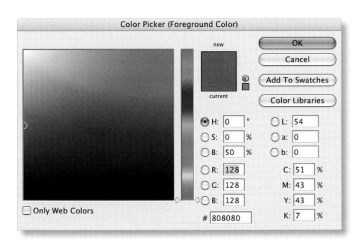

Continue painting with black or white to simulate dodging and burning. Since you're doing it all on the gray layer, nothing is destructive. Setting the brush to a low opacity gives you a nice way to creatively build the effect in areas that really need it, too. Oh yeah, if you happen to dodge or burn an area that you didn't want to, just click on your Foreground color swatch in the Toolbox, set its color to 50% gray (the color of the layer) and paint over the area. The color values are R: 128, G: 128, B: 128. That'll neutralize the effect and hide all changes, since gray appears transparent anyway. Reset your brush opacity when you're done here.

BOOSTING SPECIFIC COLORS

FOR THOSE TIMES WHEN ONLY A SPECIFIC COLOR IN A PHOTO NEEDS A BOOST

Often you'll have a photo where one of the colors just doesn't stand out like it did when you took the photo. One of the benefits of a Hue/Saturation adjustment layer is that you can target specific colors with it, and not the whole photo. Plus, the ability to hide the changes with the layer mask on the adjustment layer can really help create some strong images.

STEP 1: OPEN A PHOTO WHERE ONE COLOR JUST DOESN'T STAND OUT LIKE YOU THINK IT SHOULD

Open a photo where one color just doesn't have the punch that the others do. In this example, the green ivy on the wall just isn't as green as it looked when I took the photo.

STEP 2: ADD A HUE/SATURATION ADJUSTMENT LAYER. CHOOSE THE COLOR FROM THE EDIT MENU

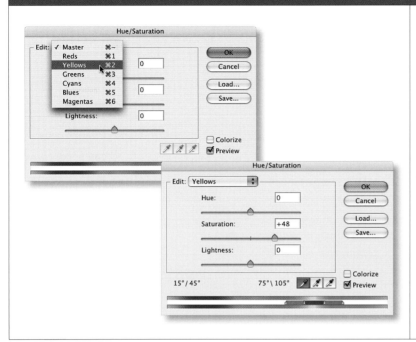

Click on the Create New Adjustment Layer icon at the bottom of the Layers panel and add a Hue/Saturation adjustment layer. From the dialog's Edit pop-up menu, choose the color that you want to boost. In this example, your gut reaction may be to choose Greens. When it comes to grass and leaves, they tend to have a lot of yellow in them, so I'm choosing Yellows here. However, it works the same for the other colors, too, so if you have something that you want more blue, choose Blue instead. Now, increase the Saturation setting and you'll see just the yellows start to become more vivid. Click OK when you're done.

STEP 3: PAINT ON THE LAYER MASK TO HIDE THE EFFECT EVERYWHERE ELSE

The problem is that anything else that was yellow/green in the photo also became more intense, and in this case the wall, water, and just about everything else became way too saturated. Since the Hue/Saturation adjustment layer has a mask on it, though, just select the Brush tool (B), choose a soft-edged brush from the Brush Picker, then press X to swap your Foreground color and make it black. Paint with black on the layer mask to hide the effects from the other areas. So now the color boost from the adjustment layer only affects the ivy and nothing else.

ENHANCING DEPTH OF FIELD

DEPTH OF FIELD IS ANOTHER GREAT WAY TO BRING MORE FOCUS TO THE SUBJECT IN A PHOTO

If you haven't figured it out yet, this chapter is all about trying to make the subject of a photo look better. That's really one of the main things we're after when enhancing digital photos. We want to make the photo look like it did when we were there. Depth of field is another way to do just that by blurring the background. For example, if you were looking at—or photographing—a beautiful flower, you'd be concentrating on its beauty, not the background. However, when that photo is developed on the computer and you see it onscreen, sometimes that background is what sticks out. This technique will help you fix that.

STEP 1: START OUT WITH A PHOTO THAT HAS A BUSY BACKGROUND THAT IS TOO IN FOCUS

Open a photo that has a busy background in it. Something where the subject is very clear, but the background is too in focus, so it really just distracts from the rest of the image. Most of the time, you can shoot with a large aperture setting in the camera to try to get this effect, but sometimes it's just not feasible. You'll also see that point-and-shoot cameras tend to bring everything into focus, too.

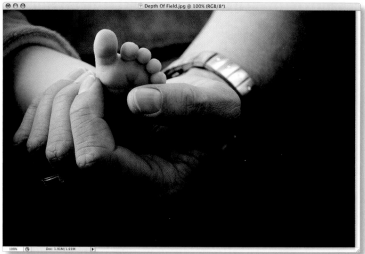

MATT KLOSKOWSKI

STEP 2: DUPLICATE THE BACKGROUND LAYER AND APPLY A GAUSSIAN BLUR FILTER

Duplicate the Background layer by pressing Command-J (PC: Ctrl-J). Click on the Filter menu and choose Blur>Gaussian Blur. The Radius setting really depends on your photo and how much blur you can get away with. Generally, you want to blur it enough so you can still see that something was back there, but you just can't see it in focus. I tend to stick with a setting of 4–5 pixels for low-resolution photos like this one. For high-res photos, try something around 10–15 pixels. Click OK when you're done.

STEP 3: ADD A LAYER MASK AND PAINT WITH BLACK TO REVEAL THE UNBLURRED BABY'S FOOT

Once again, click on the Add Layer Mask icon at the bottom of the Layers panel to add a layer mask to the blurred layer. Then, select the Brush tool (B) and choose a soft-edged brush from the Brush Picker. Make sure your Foreground color is set to black, and start painting the unblurred version of the main subject back in. Depending on what your subject is, you may need to make the brush smaller and zoom in to get the edges. Here, I had to do it to paint the area between the baby's foot and the watch and make it precise. It may take a minute or two, but it's worth the result and the effect really makes the photo look much stronger.

CREATING SOFT FOCUS

WITH A LAYER AND A FILTER, IT'S EASY TO CREATE THE EFFECT OF A TRADITIONAL PHOTOGRAPHY FILTER

I love to re-create the effect of traditional filters used in photography. The main reason is that I don't have to make the decision about a certain effect when I'm taking the photo. I know I can achieve just as good a result after the fact in Photoshop. That way, I'm not stuck with an effect that I don't want later.

STEP 1: OPEN A PHOTO THAT WOULD BENEFIT FROM A SOFT FOCUS EFFECT

Start by opening a photo that would look nice if a soft focus filter had been used when you were taking the photo. Not every photo will work for this. It's probably not good to use a photo of a pair of horses captured neck-and-neck at the finish line. That's not a "soft" photo. Portraits of people (couples, or a parent with a child) and early morning photos usually work well, though.

©ISTOCKPHOTO

STEP 2: DUPLICATE THE BACKGROUND LAYER AND APPLY THE GAUSSIAN BLUR FILTER

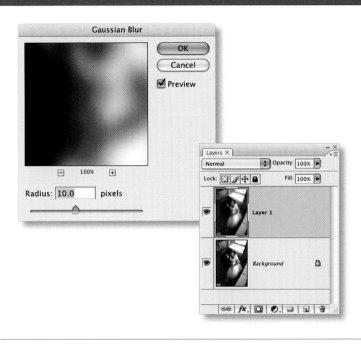

Press Command-J (PC: Ctrl-J) to duplicate the Background layer. Click on the Filter menu and choose Blur>Gaussian Blur. I usually go with a setting of 10 pixels for the Radius, but I'll tell you what to look for when applying the effect: you want to blur the whole photo, but you don't want to blur it to the point where you can't recognize anything in the photo. So, make sure you can still make out the details in the photo before you settle on a Radius setting. Click OK when you're done.

STEP 3: REDUCE THE OPACITY OF THE BLURRED LAYER TO REVEAL THE SHARP LAYER BELOW

After you run the filter, the whole photo will look blurry. The first thing to do is reduce the opacity of the blurred layer. I typically drop it down to around 50%–60%. This reveals more of the sharp layer that is below.

STEP 4: OPTIONAL: ADD A LAYER MASK AND PAINT WITH A LOW-OPACITY BLACK BRUSH

This part is optional, and really depends on your photo and whether you want to make some areas sharp again. If so, click on the Add Layer Mask icon at the bottom of the Layers panel, then select the Brush tool (B) and set the brush's Opacity setting to 30% in the Options Bar. Press X to change your Foreground color to black, and paint over the main subject in the photo to make it a little sharper than everything else. At this point, you're really done with the soft-focus effect. However, read on if you want to add a nice finishing touch to it.

STEP 5: FINISHING TOUCH: ADD A PHOTO FILTER ADJUSTMENT LAYER TO WARM THE PHOTO

A nice finishing touch for this effect is to warm the photo a bit. It gives the appearance that the photo was taken in that nice, early morning light. Click on the Create New Adjustment Layer icon at the bottom of the Layers panel, and choose Photo Filter. Choose Warming Filter (81) from the Filter pop-up menu, and increase the Density setting to 40%. Click OK and you're done. With only two extra layers, you've got a really nice way to enhance your photos.

HOW DO I...

? QUICKLY DUPLICATE A LAYER?

I know I sound like a broken record, but if there is one keyboard shortcut to get from this whole book, this is it. Press Command-J (PC: Ctrl-J) to quickly duplicate a layer.

? MAKE MY BRUSH SOFTER WITHOUT USING THE BRUSH PICKER?

To make your brush harder or softer without going to the Brush Picker, press Shift-[(Left Bracket key) or Shift-] (Right Bracket key).

? SET MY FOREGROUND AND BACKGROUND COLORS TO THEIR DEFAULTS (BLACK AND WHITE)?

Just press the letter D to set the Foreground and Background colors to their defaults of black and white. However, if you're working on a layer mask, it's the opposite. Pressing D sets white as the Foreground color and black as the Background color.

? SWAP THE FOREGROUND AND BACKGROUND COLORS WITH EACH OTHER?

Press the letter X.

? CREATE A NEW LAYER?

To quickly create a new blank layer with no dialogs popping up, press Command-Option-Shift-N (PC: Ctrl-Alt-Shift-N).

? QUICKLY CHANGE TO THE OVERLAY BLEND MODE?

Press Option-Shift-O (PC: Alt-Shift-O). If you are using a tool with a blend mode in the Options Bar, this will change the mode there. If you are using a tool without a blend mode in the Options Bar, this will change the current layer's blend mode.

? AUTOMATICALLY REAPPLY A FILTER WITH THE SAME SETTINGS?

You can automatically reapply the *last* filter you ran, with the same exact settings, by pressing Command-F (PC: Ctrl-F). You won't even see the dialog.

? AUTOMATICALLY REAPPLY A FILTER WITH DIFFERENT SETTINGS?

You can automatically reapply the *last* filter you ran, but this time see the dialog so you can adjust the settings, by pressing Command-Option-F (PC: Ctrl-Alt-F).

CHAPTER SEVEN

RETOUCHING WITH LAYERS

This is one of my favorite topics when it comes to working with layers. It's probably because there is so much you can do with some simple retouching tools and just a couple of layers. Now, as you read this chapter, keep in mind one thing: this isn't meant to be a one-stop shop for all of your retouching needs. Instead, I'd like to show you how to put some of the layer functions that you've seen already to a different use. Plus, there are a few tools in Photoshop for retouching that have some layer-related options that you can use to make your retouching even better.

REMOVING BLEMISHES AND WRINKLES

THERE ARE A FEW RETOUCHING-SPECIFIC TOOLS IN PHOTOSHOP THAT HAVE A BUILT-IN LAYERS TRICK

When you talk to people in everyday life, you probably don't notice any blemishes or wrinkles that they may have on their faces. This is because you're concentrating (hopefully) on your discussion and interaction with them. However, when you see photos of those same people, you're more likely to notice some small imperfections on their skin. That's where the retouching tools and a couple of layers come in really handy. You can lessen the effect of a person's blemishes and wrinkles, but still be conservative and keep them looking real.

STEP 1: OPEN A PORTRAIT OF SOMEONE THAT HAS A FEW BLEMISHES OR WRINKLES TO REMOVE

Start out by opening a portrait of someone who has a few blemishes or wrinkles that you'd like to remove. If you don't have one you think will work, you can download the image I used here from the website mentioned in the introduction.

TIP: If you're going to experiment on a family member or friend, please make sure you're alone first. I've found that no one likes to see their own photo open in Photoshop.

©ISTOCKPHOTO/FRANCES WICKS

STEP 2: CREATE A NEW BLANK LAYER TO HOLD ALL OF THE RETOUCHING WE'RE ABOUT TO DO

One common theme among many of the layer-related enhancements we've done in this book is to do the work on a separate layer and then drop the layer's opacity to reduce the effect. The same thing goes here. We're going to do all of our retouching on a blank layer, in case we want to bring back some of the original skin below it. So, go ahead and click on the Create a New Layer icon at the bottom of the Layers panel to create a blank layer. You can even name this new layer "Spot Healing" if you want to, because that's what we're going to do. Double-click on the layer name to rename it.

STEP 3: SELECT THE SPOT HEALING BRUSH. TURN ON THE SAMPLE ALL LAYERS OPTION

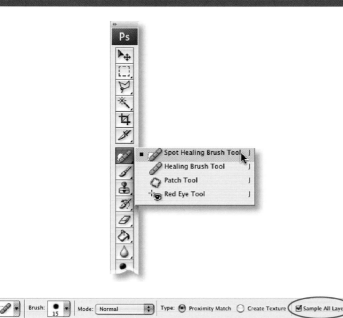

Next, select the Spot Healing Brush tool (J) from the Toolbox. Choose a very small, soft-edged brush that is no larger than the size of the spots or blemishes you're about to remove. Now, there is one key setting that makes this layer thing all work. Up in the Options Bar, you'll see a Sample All Layers checkbox. Make sure you turn this on. If you don't, then none of your work will appear on the blank layer you just created.

TIP: The Spot Healing Brush is just like the regular Brush tool. It has a Diameter setting and a Hardness setting, so use it just like you would any other brush.

STEP 4: CLICK ON ANY SPOTS OR BLEMISHES IN THE PHOTO TO REMOVE THEM

First, click once on the Spot Healing layer to make sure it's selected. The way the Spot Healing Brush works is really easy: just click on any spots or blemishes that you want to remove. That's it! Just click, and watch the spots disappear. Pretty cool, isn't it?

STEP 5: TOGGLE THE SPOT HEALING LAYER ON/OFF TO SEE THE CHANGES. REDUCE THE OPACITY

After you're done, make sure that all of your work was being done on the blank layer by showing and hiding the layer. Just click the little Eye icon next to the layer thumbnail to turn it on and off. If you happened to have removed a mole or birthmark and want to bring it back partially, just drop the Opacity setting of the Spot Healing layer a little. That will reveal the original photo below.

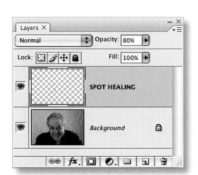

STEP 6: CREATE A NEW LAYER. SELECT THE HEALING BRUSH TOOL AND SET TO SAMPLE ALL LAYERS

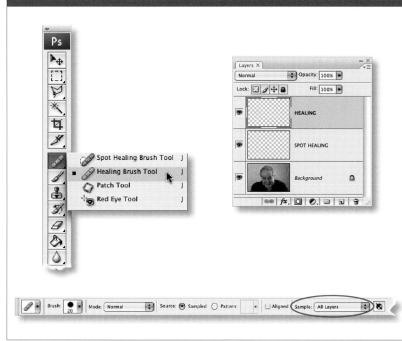

Create another new layer and name it "Healing." Now, let's move on to some heavier work—the wrinkles. The Spot Healing Brush works great on those small blemishes, but we need to bring in the big guns for the larger areas, like wrinkles and lines. Select the Healing Brush tool from the Tool-box, or press Shift-J. The Healing Brush also has a Sample All Layers option, but it's in the Sample pop-up menu in the Options Bar. Make sure you choose All Layers.

STEP 7: OPTION-CLICK (PC: ALT-CLICK) ON A CLEAR PART OF THE SKIN TO SET IT AS A SAMPLE POINT

The Healing Brush works a little differently than it's little brother, the Spot Healing Brush. With the Spot Healing Brush, you didn't have to sample anything. It just melded the spots with the sur-rounding area. The Healing Brush is different. You have to set a sample point first. This is typically some area of clear skin that is near the area you want to retouch. It doesn't have to be perfectly clean, but better than the wrinkles you want to fix. So, press-and-hold the Option (PC: Alt) key and click on a clear area of skin to serve as the sample point.

STEP 8: PAINT OVER THE WRINKLES WITH THE HEALING BRUSH TO MELD THE SAMPLE AND REAL SKIN

On the Healing layer, paint over the wrinkles or lines just as you would with any brush. Use a brush size that isn't much larger than the actual wrinkle or line itself. Use multiple strokes to continue painting on the wrinkles. Every time you let go of your mouse button, Photoshop will meld the clear, sampled area with the skin you're painting over. You'll see a little crosshair that follows your brush. That is Photoshop's way of telling you where it is sampling from. Most of the time it does a great job, but if you're not happy with a brush stroke, just press Command-Z (PC: Ctrl-Z) to Undo and try again.

STEP 9: DROP THE OPACITY OF EITHER THE SPOT HEALING BRUSH OR HEALING BRUSH LAYER

If you've never used the Healing Brush before, you're probably pretty amazed right now. I don't know how it does it, but the behind-the-scenes work that Photoshop is doing is phenomenal.

Now, the last thing to do is drop the opacity of the Healing layer. It's actually more important here than it was with the Spot Healing layer. The removed wrinkles look really fake, but by dropping the layer opacity down to around 40%–50%, you can strike a good balance between real and fake. In the end, you'll have a nice, tastefully retouched portrait.

SMOOTHING AND ENHANCING SKIN

RETOUCHING IS HOT THESE DAYS, AND ONE OF THE FIRST THINGS THAT YOU'LL DO IS SMOOTH THE SKIN

Smoothing skin helps portraits of people of all ages. It's got a few uses: First, you can use it to remove some of the texture that makeup can often leave. Next, you can use it to lessen the effect of sun lines and wrinkles.

STEP 1: OPEN A PORTRAIT WHERE THE SKIN ON THE FACE NEEDS SOME SMOOTHING

Open a portrait of a person that you'd like to try the skin-smoothing technique on. Read Steps 2 and 3 if you're going to use the same photo that you used in the previous tutorial. I'll show you how to start combining multiple techniques and still manage your layers in your Layers panel. However, if you're starting from scratch, then you can skip to Step 4.

MATT KLOSKOWSKI

STEP 2: WHAT TO DO WHEN YOU ALREADY HAVE LAYERS IN YOUR PHOTO

If you're reading this step, then I assume you're looking to bring these techniques together. Meaning: you did the first tutorial in this chapter ("Removing Blemishes and Wrinkles") and you have two extra layers on top of your Background layer already. Now you want to apply this "Smoothing and Enhancing Skin" technique, but you don't want to flatten your other layers. So, at the point of starting this tutorial, your Layers panel should look something like the one here (this is how we finished in the first tutorial).

STEP 3: FLATTEN YOUR LAYERS WITHOUT FLATTENING EVERYTHING

In order to move forward and apply other techniques, you'd probably think you have to flatten your layers. You do. But there's a better way than just choosing Layer>Flatten Image. Instead, there's a little-known keyboard shortcut that flattens your layers onto a new layer on top of everything else in the Layers panel. Here's what to do: Click on the top-most layer. Then press Command-Option-Shift-E (PC: Ctrl-Alt-Shift-E). It's called Stamp Visible Layers, and it stamps everything that is visible onto a new layer on top of all the others. It lets you flatten to a new layer, but keeps all of your other layers intact. Do this after each technique to give yourself a way out of a technique.

STEP 4: DUPLICATE THE BACKGROUND LAYER

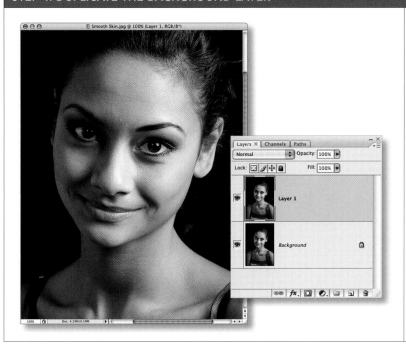

If you came here from Step 1, then you should just have a Background layer. In that case, press Command-J (PC: Ctrl-J) to duplicate the Background layer, so now there should be two copies of the same layer in the Layers panel.

However, if you came here from Step 3, then you have a flattened layer on top of several other layers. Think of this as the "new" Background layer and duplicate it just like you would the normal Background layer.

STEP 5: APPLY THE SURFACE BLUR FILTER TO THE DUPLICATE

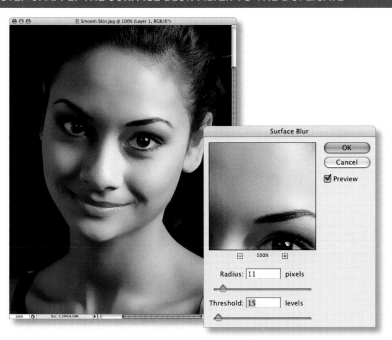

Click on the top copy in the Layers panel to make sure it's selected. In order to smooth the skin, we'll have to blur it. A lot of people go straight for the Gaussian Blur filter for this, but I like the Surface Blur filter a lot more. It leaves me with less work to do later (you'll see how in a minute). So, click the Filter menu and choose Blur>Surface Blur. Enter 11 pixels for the Radius and set the Threshold to 15. Click OK when you're done.

STEP 6: ADD A LAYER MASK TO THE BLURRED LAYER

Now you've blurred the whole photo and the skin should look really smooth. Too smooth, though, right? At this point, it looks very fake. Plus, while the Surface Blur filter does a better job than Gaussian Blur of maintaining the detail areas and just blurring the "surface" or smooth areas, it's not perfect. We still need to bring back those key sharp areas. That's where a layer mask comes in. Click on the Add Layer Mask icon at the bottom of the Layers panel to add a layer mask to the blurred layer.

STEP 7: SELECT THE BRUSH TOOL AND CHOOSE A MEDIUM-SIZED, SOFT-EDGED BRUSH

Now select the Brush tool from the Toolbox (or just press the letter B). Click on the brush thumbnail in the Options Bar and select a medium-sized, soft-edged brush from the Brush Picker (something small enough to paint inside the key feature areas, like the eyes and mouth).

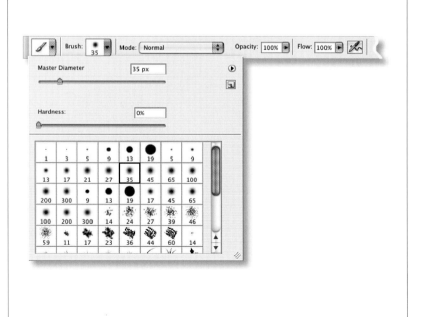

STEP 8: PAINT WITH BLACK ON THE LAYER MASK TO REVEAL THE KEY FEATURES FROM BELOW

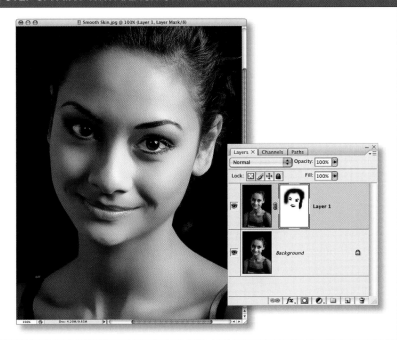

Press D, then X to set your Foreground color to black. Start painting on the photo on the main features that we want to be sharp. The eyes are the first place to start. Then move on to the nose, the mouth, and any jewelry and hair that should stay sharp, too. Don't forget that you can press the Left and Right Bracket keys to resize your brush quickly.

STEP 9: DROP THE OPACITY OF THE BLURRED LAYER TO MAKE THE SKIN LOOK MORE REALISTIC

The last step is optional, but probably recommended depending on how much you blurred the skin. See, some people like that really smooth, porcelain skin. It's very common in glamour magazines. However, I'm usually not working for a glamour magazine and I'm not a huge fan of that super-smooth look. So, I drop the Opacity setting of the blurred layer on top to around 50%–60%. That usually still does a good job of smoothing the skin, but also shows some of the original skin texture from the layer below.

MAKING EYES AND TEETH WHITER

THERE'S ONE ADJUSTMENT THAT TAKES CARE OF TWO VERY COMMON RETOUCHING TASKS

By nature, especially as we age, our eyes tend to get a little darker (and maybe even bloodshot) and our teeth start to take on a yellowish color. It's natural, but there are a few ways that you can lessen those effects in Photoshop and make someone look their very best. Even better, there's one adjustment that can take care of both tasks so you can be done with as little as two extra layers.

STEP 1: OPEN A PHOTO WHERE THE EYES OR TEETH NEED WHITENING

All right, start out by opening a photo where the eyes or teeth need whitening. Or both, if you have one. This photo can actually use a little of both adjustments, but we'll work on one area at a time. If you've already done some retouching like we did in the previous two tutorials in this chapter, then you already have some layers. If you want to save those layers, then use the trick mentioned in Step 3 of the previous technique to flatten your image onto a new layer on top. That'll be your New Background layer (seen here). If not, then just start out with the Background layer.

If you're combining multiple techniques, merge to a new layer

If not, then just start with the Background layer

MATT KLOSKOWSKI

STEP 2: ADD A HUE/SATURATION ADJUSTMENT LAYER, CHOOSE REDS, AND REDUCE THE SATURATION

First, let's work on the eyes. Click on the Create New Adjustment Layer icon at the bottom of the Layers panel and add a Hue/Saturation adjustment layer. One of the common problems with eyes is that they tend to have some red in them. So choose Reds from the Edit pop-up menu at the top and reduce the Saturation setting. I know, things get pretty scary-looking at this point, but don't worry. We'll fix it in a minute.

STEP 3: SWITCH BACK TO MASTER AND INCREASE THE LIGHTNESS SETTING

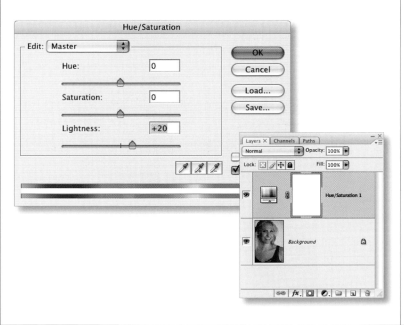

Switch back to the Master setting under the Edit pop-up menu. Increase the Lightness setting to 20 to lighten the whole photo. Click OK when you're done.

STEP 4: FILL THE MASK WITH BLACK. USE THE BRUSH TOOL TO PAINT WITH WHITE ON THE EYES

Since the whole photo looks really bad and we just want to fix a small area, let's fill the adjustment layer mask with black. Just press Command-I (PC: Ctrl-I) to invert the white and make it black. That hides the Hue/Saturation adjustment. Now, use the Zoom tool (Z) to zoom in on the eyes. Press D to set your Foreground to white, select the Brush tool (B) and paint with white over the whites of her eyes. You'll probably have to use a small brush and take your time, but it should only take a minute or so. When you're done, drop the adjustment layer's opacity to around 80% to make the whiter eyes more believable.

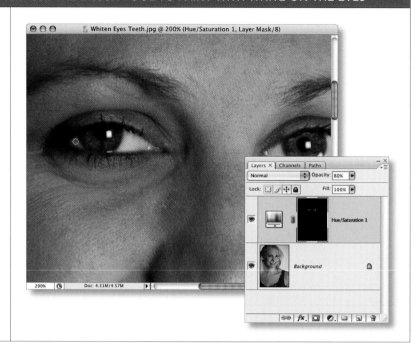

STEP 5: MOVE ON TO THE TEETH FOR WHITENING. MAKE A SELECTION OF THE TEETH FIRST

Now, let's move on to the teeth. This time, let's make a selection first. Select the teeth with your favorite selection tool. I used the Quick Selection tool (W) for this photo and just clicked on the teeth until they were all selected. Don't worry if you get a little of the gums in there, we'll fix that later. Just make sure you get all the teeth.

STEP 6: ADD ANOTHER HUE/SATURATION ADJUSTMENT FOR THE TEETH. THIS TIME, CHOOSE YELLOWS

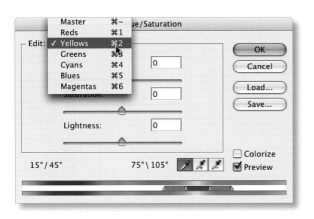

Add another Hue/Saturation adjustment layer. This time choose Yellows from the Edit pop-up menu at the top.

STEP 7: DRAG THE SATURATION TO THE LEFT. GO BACK TO MASTER AND INCREASE LIGHTNESS

Bring the Saturation setting all the way to the left. Just like before, switch the Edit pop-up menu back to Master, and increase the Lightness setting—just a little—to around 10. Notice how the adjustment is just being restricted to the area we selected back in Step 5. Click OK when you're done. You'll also see that, even though we have two Hue/Saturation adjustment layers on top of each other, the changes aren't being applied to the whole photo. That's because the layer masks each allow the adjustment layer to show only a small part of the adjustment (eyes and teeth).

STEP 8: USE THE BRUSH TOOL TO TWEAK THE LAYER MASK IN CASE THE SELECTION WASN'T PERFECT

Once again, select the Brush tool (B) and use the Zoom tool (Z) to zoom in on the teeth. Make sure your Foreground color is white, and paint on any areas that may not have gotten selected the first time. Or, press X to switch your Foreground and Background colors, and paint with black to hide the changes from areas that your selection may have spilled over into accidentally. Drop the opacity of the Hue/Saturation adjustment layer if the teeth start to look too white. Now you have whitened the eyes and the teeth with just two layers.

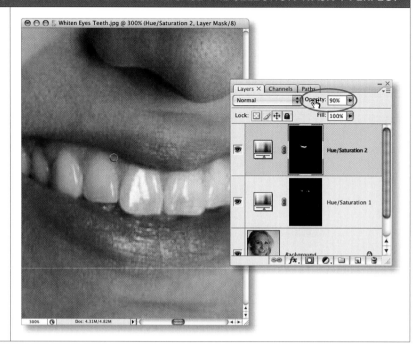

REMOVING DISTRACTIONS

RETOUCHING ISN'T RESTRICTED TO PEOPLE. STILL LIFE, OUTDOOR, AND LANDSCAPE PHOTOS CAN ALSO BENEFIT

The Clone Stamp tool can be your best friend when working on landscape photos. In fact, just about every landscape and still life photo can use a quick once-over with the Clone Stamp tool, as well as some other minor retouching to remove distractions. Just like the healing tools we saw earlier in the chapter, the Clone Stamp tool also has a special layers-related function.

STEP 1: OPEN A PHOTO WITH SOME DISTRACTIONS THAT NEED TO BE REMOVED

Open a photo with some distractions or unwanted areas in it. Here's a shot I took in Brugge, Belgium. I like the photo a lot, but it's got these little black vertical bars on the brick wall next to the windows that are distracting. We'll use the Clone Stamp tool to remove them.

MATT KLOSKOWSKI

STEP 2: CREATE A NEW LAYER TO HOLD THE RETOUCHING WORK WE'RE ABOUT TO DO

Just like we did when retouching the portraits, click on the Create a New Layer icon at the bottom of the Layers panel to create a new blank layer to hold our retouching work.

STEP 3: GET THE CLONE STAMP TOOL. MAKE SURE SAMPLE ALL LAYERS IS SELECTED

Select the Clone Stamp tool from the Toolbox, or press the letter S to get it. The Clone Stamp tool is a lot like the Healing Brush tool. It's got the same Sample pop-up menu in the Options Bar. Make sure you choose Sample All Layers from this pop-up menu so we can do our work on the blank layer. Otherwise, when we sample a point with the Clone Stamp tool, it'll just sample from the transparent layer (which has nothing on it).

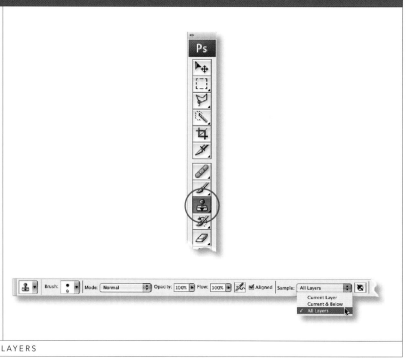

STEP 4: OPTION-CLICK (PC: ALT-CLICK) ON A CLEAN AREA TO SET IT AS A SAMPLE POINT

I mentioned that the Clone Stamp tool is a lot like the Healing Brush. So much so that you've got to set a sample point with it just like we did in the Healing Brush tutorial. You've got to be a little more careful when setting the sample point with the Clone Stamp tool, though. It doesn't meld areas together like the Healing Brush; it copies them exactly. So you'll want to sample an area that's close to what you're going to be cloning. Option-click (PC: Alt-click) on the brick area directly next to one of the black bars to set it as the clone sample point. Use the Zoom tool (Z) to zoom in, if necessary.

STEP 5: PAINT OVER THE UNWANTED AREA NEXT TO THE POINT YOU SAMPLED FROM

Click on the brush thumbnail in the Options Bar and choose a small, soft-edged brush in the Brush Picker. Click-and-drag to paint downward over the black bar. Again, you'll see that little crosshair following your cursor, showing you where Photoshop is sampling from.

TIP: If you're having a hard time getting the bricks to match up, try to remember exactly where you sampled (Option-clicked) from. Then, when you start to paint (or clone) on the bricks, start your brush stroke on the same line you sampled from. That should help align the bricks you clone with the ones that you're sampling from.

STEP 6: OPTION-CLICK AGAIN IN ANOTHER PART OF THE PHOTO TO SET ANOTHER SAMPLE POINT

Since the Clone Stamp tool is a little more finicky than the Healing Brush, we're going to set another sample point. If we don't, we're likely to pull the color and texture from the first part of the wall we sampled to a different area where we'll clone next. Option-click (PC: Alt-click) on another point right next to the next black bar you're going to remove. Then, click-and-drag with the Clone Stamp tool along the bar to clone it away.

STEP 7: CONTINUE CLONING ALL OF THE DARK BLACK LINES OUT OF THE PHOTO

Continue this process throughout the photo. The closer you can sample to the area you're going to clone away, the better results you're going to get.

One more thing (those of you with keen eyes out there already figured this out, I bet): You're saying, "What about the reflection?" Don't forget to move down to the reflection in the water and do the same thing. (Here, you can see the Clone Stamp cursor just below the building beneath the rounded window.) You thought you got me on that one, didn't you?

STEP 8: YOU DON'T ALWAYS HAVE TO USE THE CLONE STAMP TOOL. TRY THE SPOT HEALING BRUSH

You'll notice a few black drain holes toward the bottom of the photo. There's no rule that states you have to use the Clone Stamp tool all the time. Earlier in the chapter we used the Spot Healing Brush on a portrait, but it'll work great in this circumstance, too. Give it a try. Select the Spot Healing Brush (J) and make sure Sample All Layers is still turned on. Then click on those black spots to remove them.

STEP 9: ONCE AGAIN, YOUR RETOUCHING IS ALL DONE ON A SEPARATE LAYER

Just like everything else we've done in this chapter, your retouching in this exercise is all on its own layer. This comes in really handy because you can go back to this layer and erase, enhance, or change one specific part of your retouching work without affecting the rest of it. If you did the work all on the photo layer, then you'd have to undo *all* of your work just to get back to a point earlier. Now, you can specifically change something without starting from scratch.

HOW DO I...

? DO MY RETOUCHING ON A BLANK LAYER?

To retouch on a blank layer, make sure you select the Sample All Layers option in the Options Bar for the tool you're using (this works for the Spot Healing Brush, the Healing Brush, and the Clone Stamp tool). Then, create a blank layer and make sure it's selected when you're retouching.

? LESSEN THE EFFECT OF ANY RETOUCHING I'VE DONE ON A LAYER?

The best way to lessen any retouching effect is to do the retouching on a separate blank layer and then reduce the opacity of that layer to bring in the original texture, pattern, or object from the layer below.

? FLATTEN MY LAYERS WITHOUT ACTUALLY FLATTENING THEM?

This is one of my favorite little tricks. Flattening without flattening is very useful. Say you want to work on a flattened layer of the work you've done thus far, but you don't want to actually flatten all of the layers in your Layers panel. Click on the top layer in your Layers panel. Then, press Command-Option-Shift-E (PC: Ctrl-Alt-Shift-E). This creates a new layer and stamps all of the layers under it onto that new layer. But, it leaves all the layers intact so they're not actually flattened.

? QUICKLY SWITCH TO YELLOWS IN THE HUE/SATURATION ADJUSTMENT DIALOG?

Just press Command-2 (PC: Ctrl-2). In fact, all of the colors in the Hue/Saturation adjustment dialog have a shortcut key. They range from Command-1 (PC: Ctrl-1) through Command-6 (PC: Ctrl-6) (just check the Edit pop-up menu for the rest).

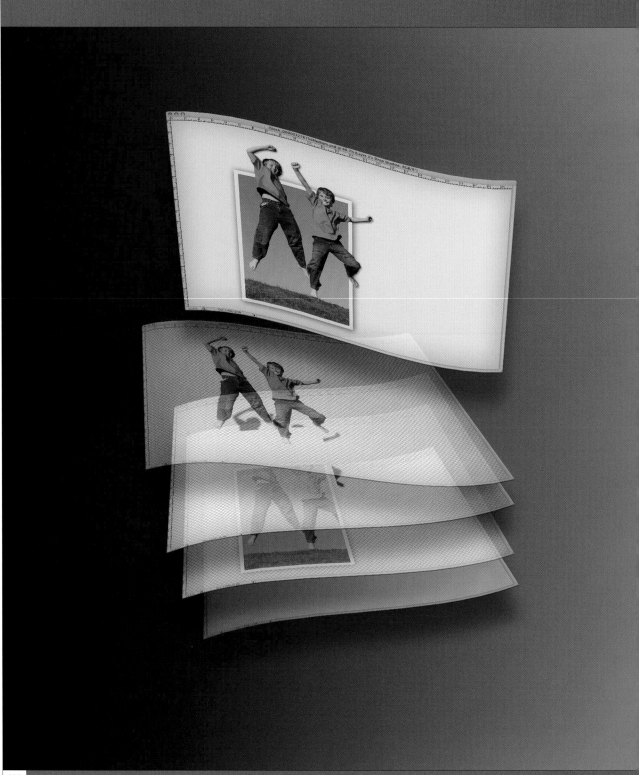

LAYER STYLES

Photoshop has a bunch of layer effects (known as Layer Styles) such as shadows, glows, bevels, and strokes that can be instantly applied to any layer. That, in and of itself, is a great time saver. However, layer styles take it a step further in two ways: 1) You can always edit them. They're live effects, so you can add a 4-pixel white stroke around a layer and later decide to go back and make it a 2-pixel stroke instead. 2) You can save them. This lets you make a style that you really like, save it, and open another photo and apply that same style to it with just a click. There are literally thousands of combinations with layers, so roll your sleeves up and get ready to be wowed if you've never seen them in action before.

DESIGNING WITH LAYER STYLES

YOU CAN CREATE SOME REALLY EYE-CATCHING DESIGNS WITH A FEW SIMPLE LAYER STYLES

The beauty of layer styles is their simplicity. They're easy to add, easy to save, and easy to change (if you ever need to). Plus, they're built right into Photoshop. Effects that used to be a total pain in the neck to add to an image are now just a click away. Drop shadows, strokes, glows, bevels…the whole nine yards. I'm tellin' ya, if you haven't messed around with layer styles for design purposes yet, then you owe it to yourself to read this tutorial, and the rest of the chapter.

STEP 1: OPEN A PHOTO TO APPLY AN EFFECT TO

Open a photo to apply a layer style design effect to. I've found they work great on people and sports photos. If you want to follow along using this same image, go to the book's download website listed in the introduction.

©ISTOCKPHOTO

STEP 2: SELECT THE BOYS FROM THE BACKGROUND AND PUT THEM ON THEIR OWN LAYER

First things first. You have to select your main subject off of the photo's background. Here, I've used the Quick Selection tool (W) to put a selection around the two boys, but feel free to use whatever selection tool you're most comfortable with. After you make the selection, press Command-J (PC: Ctrl-J) to put the selection up onto its own layer.

STEP 3: MAKE A RECTANGULAR SELECTION OF THE BACKGROUND AREA YOU WANT TO INCLUDE

Click on the Background layer again to select it. Then use the Rectangular Marquee tool (M) to make a rectangular selection around the part of the photo you want to keep. Make sure the selection includes part of the two boys. That way, they'll appear to be jumping out of the photo later. Once again, press Command-J (PC: Ctrl-J) to put this rectangular selection up onto its own layer.

STEP 4: CLICK ON THE ADD A LAYER STYLE ICON AT THE BOTTOM OF THE LAYERS PANEL

Click on the rectangular photo layer that you just made in the previous step. We're going to put a stroke around the photo, but in a different way than we've done it in this book so far. At the bottom of the Layers panel, you'll see the *fx* icon. This is the Add a Layer Style icon. Click on it to see the pop-up menu of layer styles that you can add.

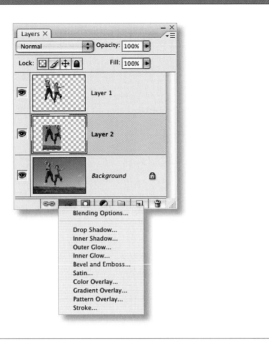

STEP 5: ADD A STROKE LAYER STYLE

Choose Stroke from the pop-up menu to open the Layer Style dialog. You'll see that Stroke is already chosen on the left, and the Stroke settings are open. Change the Size to 20 pixels. Set the Position to Inside. Finally, next to Color at the bottom, click on the color swatch and change the color to white.

TIP: Setting the Position to Inside makes the stroke edges crisp instead of rounded.

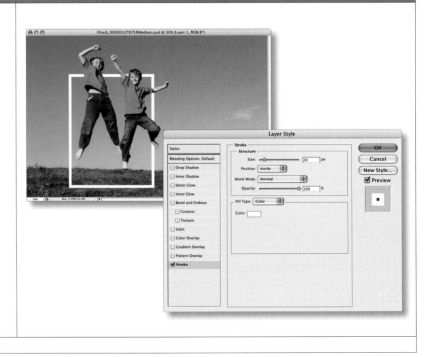

STEP 6: ADD AN OUTER GLOW LAYER STYLE TO LIFT THE SELECTION OFF THE BACKGROUND

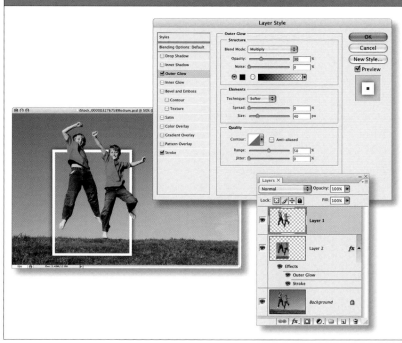

Click on Outer Glow on the left of the Layer Style dialog to add an outer glow layer style to the layer, too. Here's a tip, though. Make sure you don't just turn on the checkbox, but actually click on the words "Outer Glow" to see the right settings. In the Structure section at the top, click on the color swatch and change the color from yellow to black. Then change the blend mode from Screen to Multiply. This puts a dark edge around the photo, almost like a shadow. Increase the Size setting to 40 pixels and reduce the Opacity to 30%. Click OK to close the dialog. You'll be able to see the styles in the Layers panel.

STEP 7: ADD A DROP SHADOW LAYER STYLE TO THE LAYER WITH THE BOYS JUMPING ON IT

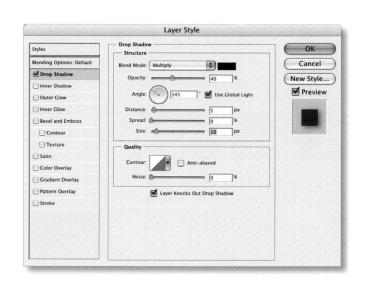

Now let's add a layer style to the layer with the boys jumping. This time, double-click on the layer thumbnail to open the Layer Style dialog. Click on Drop Shadow on the left to see the settings. Reduce the Opacity to 40% to soften the shadow. Change the Angle setting to 145° and the Size to 10 pixels. Click OK when you're done. Now the boys have a shadow below them, too. However, this shadow not only falls on the outside of the photo but on the inside, as well. We'll take care of that in Step 11.

STEP 8: FILL THE BACKGROUND LAYER WITH WHITE TO BETTER SEE THE OVERALL IMAGE

To make things easier to see and more pleasing overall, click on the Background layer and fill it with white. To do this, press D to set your Background color to white, then press Command-Delete (PC: Ctrl-Backspace) to fill the layer with your Background color. This gives a nice backdrop for the "breaking out of the photo" effect we're creating.

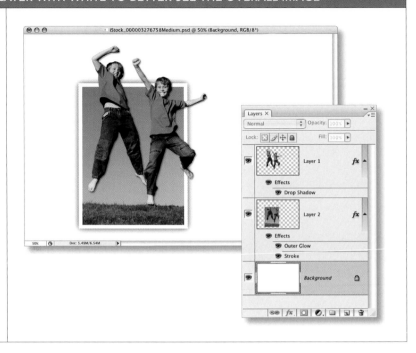

STEP 9: COPY THE DROP SHADOW LAYER STYLE FROM ONE LAYER TO ANOTHER

One trick with layer styles is copying them. For example, we applied an Outer Glow layer style to the rectangular photo to simulate a shadow below it. However, let's say you like the Drop Shadow layer style better. You can copy it from one layer to another. Just press-and-hold the Option (PC: Alt) key and click-and-drag the Drop Shadow layer style from one layer to another. Release your mouse button over the layer with the outer glow on it and you'll see the Drop Shadow layer style gets copied over.

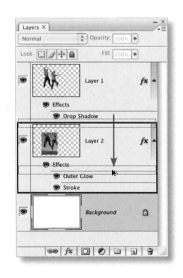

STEP 10: HIDE ONLY THE OUTER GLOW LAYER STYLE

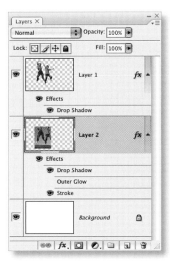

Since we don't need two shadows on the rectangular photo layer, click on the little Eye icon next to the Outer Glow layer style to hide just that layer style, but still see the Drop Shadow layer style.

TIP: If you want to delete the outer glow altogether, just click on the Outer Glow layer style in the Layers panel and drag it onto the Trash icon at the bottom of the panel.

STEP 11: TURN THE DROP SHADOW LAYER STYLE INTO A REGULAR LAYER

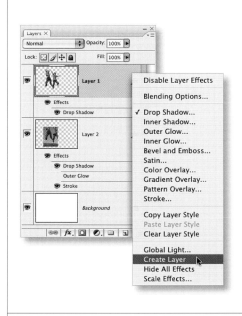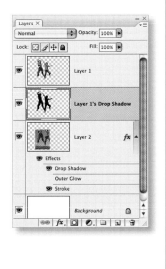

One problem that is left with this image is that the shadow behind the two boys is unrealistic. See, it should indeed fall on the area outside the rectangular photo. That's what gives the effect of them "breaking out" of the photo. However, there shouldn't be a shadow on top of the photo itself. To fix this, we need to turn the effects of the layer style into a regular layer. Control-click (PC: Right-click) on the *fx* icon on the right side of the layer. From the contextual menu, choose Create Layer. This renders the layer style to its own layer below the two boys. It's not an editable layer style anymore, but we can go in and erase from it now.

STEP 12: ERASE AWAY THE UNWANTED AREAS FROM THE DROP SHADOW

Make sure you have the drop shadow layer selected, then select the Eraser tool (E) and erase away the areas where the shadow appears over the "photo." However, leave the drop shadow wherever it extends past the white stroke edge to give the appearance that the boys are indeed breaking out of the photo.

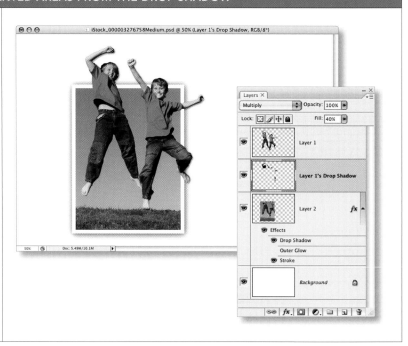

CREATING A WATERMARK

LAYER STYLES ACTUALLY HAVE TWO OPACITY SETTINGS THAT CAN BE USED FOR DIFFERENT EFFECTS

Throughout this book, we've duplicated a layer many times, applied an effect to the duplicate, and then reduced the opacity of the layer. All along we've been reducing the actual Opacity setting, but you may have seen a Fill (opacity) setting in the Layers panel, as well. Here's where you'll learn what the difference is.

STEP 1: OPEN AN IMAGE TO WATERMARK. ADD THE COPYRIGHT SYMBOL AS A CUSTOM SHAPE LAYER

Open any image that you want to protect or watermark. This technique is really useful for images you want to place on the Web, but don't want people to steal or use without paying you. The first thing you need to do is add the shape that you want to use as the watermark. It could be your company logo, your initials, or just a copyright symbol. Here, I've used the Custom Shape tool's copyright symbol. It's one of the default shapes located in the Custom Shape Picker.

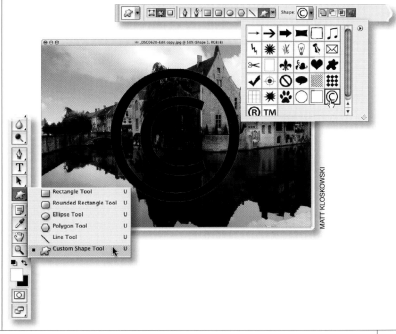

MATT KLOSKOWSKI

STEP 2: ADD A BEVEL AND EMBOSS LAYER STYLE TO THE COPYRIGHT SYMBOL LAYER

Double-click on the copyright Shape layer to open the Layer Style dialog. Click on Bevel and Emboss on the left side of the dialog to open those settings. Change the Depth setting to 250%. Click OK to close the dialog.

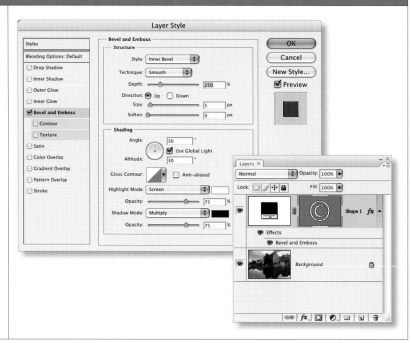

STEP 3: REDUCE THE FILL OPACITY

In order for this to work as a watermark you need to see through the black area. If you just decrease the layer's Opacity setting, you'll definitely make the black part of the shape see-through but you'll also hide the Bevel and Emboss layer style, which is key to the watermark effect. Instead, reduce the Fill setting to 0%. Doing this hides the pixels that are on the layer (in this case, the black copyright symbol shape), but leaves any layer style effects. Here, that means we see the Bevel and Emboss layer style, which is what gives the appearance of a watermark.

CREATING REUSABLE PHOTO EFFECTS

LAYER STYLES ARE GREAT FOR CREATING EYE-CATCHING AND REUSABLE PHOTO EFFECTS

Many Photoshop users out there typically think of layer styles as a "design" effect. That is, as something that designers would use more than photographers. Honestly, that's partly true, but there are some great photographic examples of layer styles, too. In fact, they really come in handy when it comes to creating reusable photographic effects, because you create them once, save them, and then apply them to other photos with just one click. Let's take a look.

STEP 1: OPEN A PHOTO THAT YOU'D LIKE TO APPLY A CLASSIC TINT EFFECT TO

Start out by opening the photo that you're going to apply a classic tint to. Anything is fair game here, but I have a photo I took at this little outdoor museum on the side of the road outside Taos, New Mexico.

Interesting Side Story: My wife said, "Honey, you should pull over and shoot those gas pumps." Being one not to rock the boat, I said, "Sure!" To her dismay, I finally walked back to the car 45 minutes and 2 gigabytes later. Moral of this story: Never suggest photographing something to a photographer if you're not prepared to wait while they do just that.

MATT KLOSKOWSKI

STEP 2: TURN THE BACKGROUND LAYER INTO A REGULAR LAYER

One little nuance about layer styles is that you can't apply them to a Background layer. So double-click on the Background layer here and click OK to turn it into a regular layer.

STEP 3: ADD A COLOR OVERLAY LAYER STYLE AND CHANGE THE COLOR TO BROWN

Double-click the layer to open the Layer Style dialog. Click on Color Overlay on the left side. This will turn your whole photo to an ugly red (the default tint). First, click on the color swatch to the right of the Blend Mode pop-up menu, and change it to the color you want to tint your photo. I'm choosing an orangey/brown here (R: 111, G: 91, B: 51).

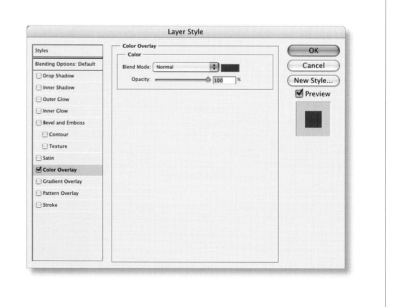

STEP 4: CHANGE THE BLEND MODE IN THE COLOR OVERLAY STYLE TO COLOR

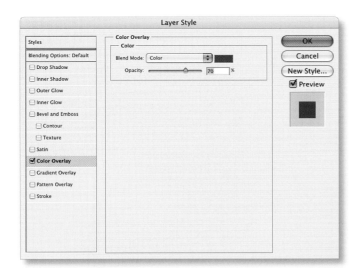

At this point, you'll still only be able to see a solid color on your photo. To see through the color, change the Blend Mode pop-up menu to Color. This uses the color you just chose to tint the overall photo. If it's too much color tint, then drop the Opacity setting to 60%–70%.

STEP 5: ADD AN INNER GLOW. CHANGE THE COLOR TO BLACK AND BLEND MODE TO MULTIPLY

To bring this effect home, click on Inner Glow on the left to show those settings. Inner Glow is set to put a yellowish glow inside your photo. But we're going to use it for an edge-darkening effect. First, click on the color swatch and change the color to black. Then, change the Blend Mode pop-up menu to Multiply. Finally, increase the Size setting to something large like 70 px (maybe higher if you have a high-res photo). It's probably going to be too much and too dark, so drop the Opacity setting down to 30%–40%. Don't click OK yet, though.

STEP 6: SAVE THE LAYER STYLE AS A REUSABLE PRESET

Take a look over at the right side of the dialog. See the New Style button? Click on that button to open the New Style dialog. Give your style a descriptive name and click OK to save it. Now you've saved this style so you can use it again later. Go ahead and click OK to close the Layer Style dialog.

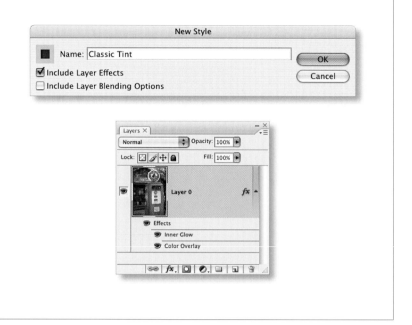

STEP 7: OPEN ANOTHER PHOTO THAT YOU'D LIKE TO APPLY THE SAME EFFECT TO

You can save-and-close the first photo now. You're done with that one. Go ahead and open another photo that you'd like to apply the same effect to. Here's another shot taken in my 45-minute (sorry, Diana—that's my wife's name, by the way) excursion.

MATT KLOSKOWSKI

STEP 8: OPEN THE STYLES PANEL. FIND THE STYLE YOU JUST CREATED

Now that you've opened another photo to apply the style to, you've got to find the style, right? Just click the Window menu and choose Styles. This opens the Styles panel. Here is where all your preset layer styles live. If you scroll to the very bottom, you'll see the Classic Tint style we just created.

TIP: If you click the arrow at the top right of the Styles panel to open the panel's flyout menu, you'll see there are lots of preset styles that Photoshop ships with, and they're all already on your computer. Give 'em a try.

STEP 9: CLICK ON THE STYLE ICON TO APPLY IT TO THE NEW PHOTO IN JUST ONE CLICK

Now just click on the Classic Tint style icon in the Styles panel to apply it to the new photo. Don't forget that it won't work until you've converted the Background layer to a regular layer.

You're pretty much done, but let's say you want to change some aspect of the style, like the color you chose in Color Overlay. Just double-click on the Color Overlay layer style's name in the Layers panel to open the Layer Style dialog to the those settings, and change the color to whatever you like. That's the cool thing about layer styles. They're live effects, meaning you can always go back and change them at any point.

SOME MORE LAYER STYLE IDEAS

HERE ARE A FEW MORE IDEAS WHEN IT COMES TO USING LAYER STYLES

I mentioned earlier that there were literally thousands of possibilities when it comes to what you can do with layer styles. There are, and I can't list them all but here are a few of my favorites.

IDEA 1: AQUA PLASTIC EFFECT

The aqua plastic effect was all the rage back in the late '90s and early 2000s, and is just as cool of an effect now. To achieve this effect, make a pill-shaped selection and fill it with white to create the Web button shape, then use the Type tool to add the text for your button. Double-click on the layer to open the Layer Style dialog, and use the settings shown here and on the next few pages.

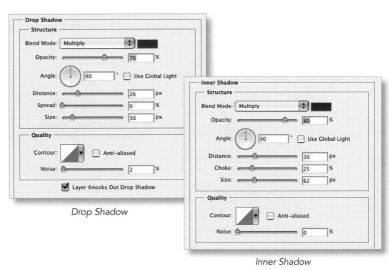

Drop Shadow

Inner Shadow

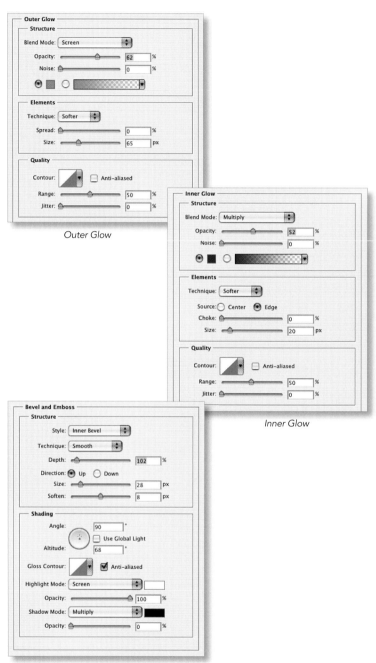

Outer Glow

Inner Glow

Bevel and Emboss

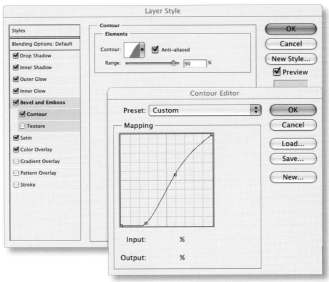

Bevel and Emboss Contour

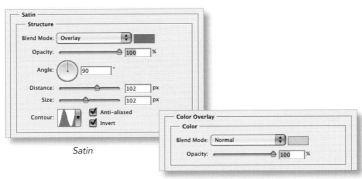

Satin

Color Overlay

Final Image

Chrome is always a cool effect. It works for everything from objects to text. Here, I've used it on a yin yang symbol. To achieve this effect, just double-click on the object, Type, or Shape layer to open the Layer Style dialog, and use the layer style settings shown here.

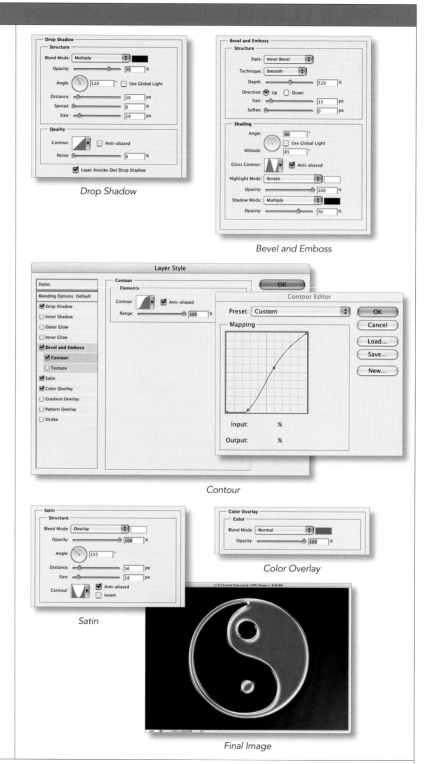

Drop Shadow

Bevel and Emboss

Contour

Satin

Color Overlay

Final Image

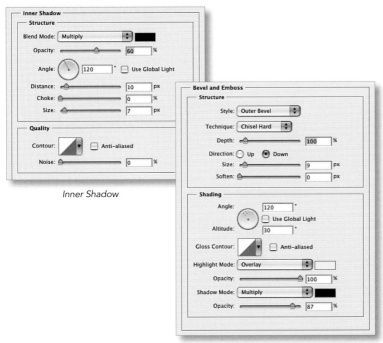

Inner Shadow

Bevel and Emboss

Layer styles are also great for making an object look like it's carved into the surface that it's on. Here I've got an image of a marble texture beneath a custom Shape layer, but it also works great on wood and steel texture backgrounds, too. To achieve this effect, double-click on the layer with your object or text on it to open the Layer Style dialog, and use the settings shown here.

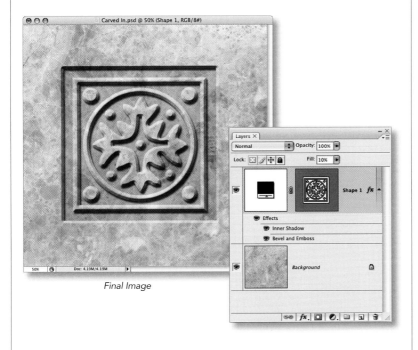

Final Image

This is one of my favorites. It looks so deceiving, like you'd need a few layers and effects to create this. Truth is, you can create a great-looking neon glow effect with just a few layer styles. The key is: it's all in the Stroke layer style. Just double-click on your Type layer to open the Layer Style dialog, and use the settings shown here.

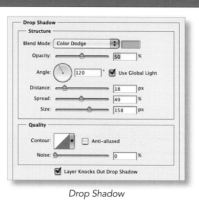

Drop Shadow

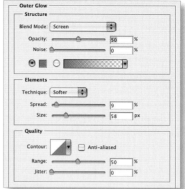

Outer Glow

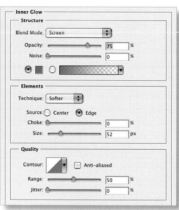

Inner Glow

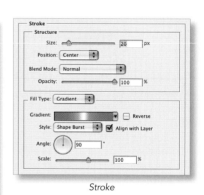

Stroke

Final Image

HOW DO I...

? ADD A LAYER STYLE TO A LAYER?

Double-click on the layer thumbnail or an open area on the layer, and that will open the Layer Style dialog.

? QUICKLY DUPLICATE A LAYER STYLE?

Press-and-hold the Option (PC: Alt) key and click-and-drag the layer style you want to duplicate to the layer you want to add it to.

? TURN OFF JUST ONE LAYER STYLE OUT OF SEVERAL THAT I'VE APPLIED TO A LAYER?

Say you've applied Drop Shadow, Bevel and Emboss, and Stroke layer styles to a layer. To turn off just the drop shadow, click on the Eye icon next to it in the Layers panel. It'll still be there, but it won't be visible anymore.

? DELETE A LAYER STYLE?

Drag the small fx icon in the Layers panel to the Trash icon at the bottom. Or, you can Control-click (PC: Right-click) on it and choose Clear Style.

? SAVE A LAYER STYLE?

In the Layer Style dialog, click on the New Style button in the top right. Give your style a descriptive name and click OK.

? SEE MY SAVED LAYER STYLES?

Your saved layer styles live in the Styles panel. Click the Window menu and choose Styles to see them.

? APPLY A SAVED LAYER STYLE?

Open the Styles panel, then select the layer you want to apply the style to in the Layers panel, and click on the style in the Styles panel to apply it.

? TURN ANY APPLIED LAYER STYLES INTO A REGULAR LAYER?

Layer styles are always editable, even after you've applied them. However, to turn them into regular layers that you can paint and erase on, just Control-click (PC: Right-click) on the layer style icon in the Layers panel and choose Create Layer(s).

? MAKE THE LIGHTING ANGLE ON ONE LAYER STYLE DIFFERENT FROM THE ANGLE ON ANOTHER?

Let's say you've added three Drop Shadow layer styles to three different layers. By default, the Angle setting will be the same for all three. If you change it for one layer, it will change for all three. To get around this, in the Layer Style dialog, turn off the Use Global Light checkbox for the layer style you're working on. That will let you change its Angle independently.

CHAPTER NINE

SMART LAYERS

In recent versions of Photoshop (CS2 and CS3), Adobe has started doing some really neat things with layers. They're beginning to make them indestructible. This means that you can now do things to layers like transforming, resizing, warping, and replacing—nondestructively. This always gives you an out and always gives you a way back, in case something in your image changes as time goes on. In Photoshop CS3, you can even apply a filter to a layer and then go back to change the filter settings at any time. So, the moral of this story is that Photoshop's layers are getting smarter and smarter. Turn the page and read this chapter to find out how.

FOUR REASONS WHY SMART OBJECTS ROCK!

SMART OBJECTS FLAT OUT ROCK! HERE ARE FOUR REASONS WHY

If you're the type who likes to learn hands-on, then feel free to skip this tutorial and jump to the next one. It's a real-world project all about Smart Objects, and showcases all of the great features that they have. However, if you just want a quick recap of what Smart Objects are and why you'd want to use them, then read this tutorial first.

STEP 1: CREATING A SMART OBJECT

Before you jump into the reasons why Smart Objects rock, you've got to know what they are and how to create them. First, a Smart Object layer is a special kind of layer that is basically indestructible. Everything you do to it is non-destructive and reversible. You'll see how in a minute. To create a Smart Object layer, click the File menu and choose Open as Smart Object. Then choose an image or photo to open. Whoa! Look at that. There are my kids again!

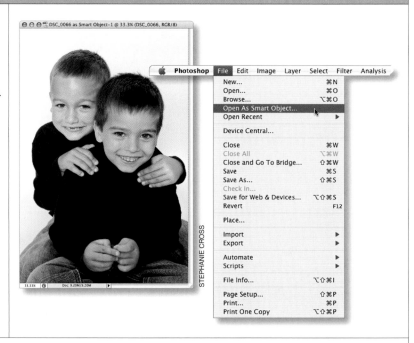

Now look over in the Layers panel. You'll see a layer there just like you'd normally expect. However, look a little closer at it and you'll notice an icon (circled here in red) in the bottom right corner of the layer thumbnail. That icon means the layer is a Smart Object layer. Everything else should still look the same. There…you've created your first Smart Object layer. Now, on to the four reasons why Smart Objects rock!

REASON 1: SMART OBJECTS = SMART FILTERS

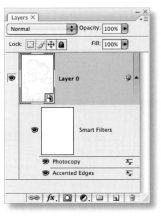

Ever hear of a nondestructive filter? Every time we've run a filter in this book, it's been a permanent change to the layer. The only way to go back and change the settings of that filter is to undo all of your changes. However, there's a nifty little feature in Photoshop CS3 called Smart Filters. It lets you run a filter on a layer (through the Filter menu, just like you normally would), then lets you go back and change it later if you need to. However, Smart Filters can only be added to Smart Object layers. So, if you didn't open your file as a Smart Object, you'd need to convert the layer to a Smart Object first.

REASON 2A: SMART OBJECTS ARE RESIZABLE

Smart Objects are also infinitely resizable. This means that you can open an image as a Smart Object (like maybe a logo). Then make it smaller. Then make it larger again. Then make it smaller and larger again, and never lose any image quality. If you tried this on a non–Smart Object layer you'd probably get something that looked like the last image you see here.

©ISTOCKPHOTO/DAR YANG YAN AND MATT KLOSKOWSKI

A regular layer loses quality when you resize it smaller then larger again

REASON 2B: SMART OBJECTS ARE RESIZABLE

However, if the layer that you're resizing is a Smart Object layer, then it will remain crisp even though you're resizing it.

A Smart Object layer remains crisp when you resize it smaller then larger again

REASON 3A: SMART OBJECTS ARE REPLACEABLE

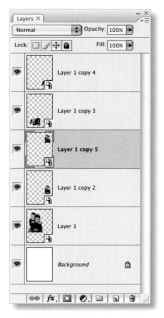

STEPHANIE CROSS

Another really cool feature of Smart Objects is that they're replaceable. Here's what it means: Let's say that you take the time to create a custom picture package layout with a single photo. Chances are you'd be duplicating, resizing, and moving several copies of the layers all over the place. Then you print it off and life is good. Now you come to the next project and want to use the same layout, but with a different photo. Without Smart Objects, you'd have to go back and change each and every layer to a different photo.

REASON 3B: SMART OBJECTS ARE REPLACEABLE

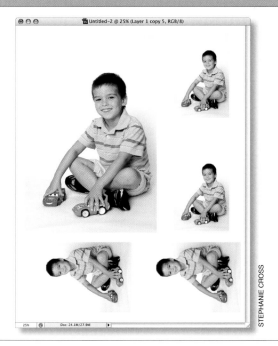

STEPHANIE CROSS

With Smart Objects layers, you just select one of the layers, click the Layer menu and choose Smart Objects>Replace Contents. Choose a different photo and all of the photos will be replaced at once, as seen here. Sweet!!!

The last really cool feature of Smart Objects is they let you work with vector artwork directly from Illustrator. Say you place several instances of a logo, which was created in Illustrator, in your image. Then you later decide you want to change some aspect of that logo—be it color or shape. Without Smart Objects, you'd have to delete your layers and start over again after you changed the logo in Illustrator.

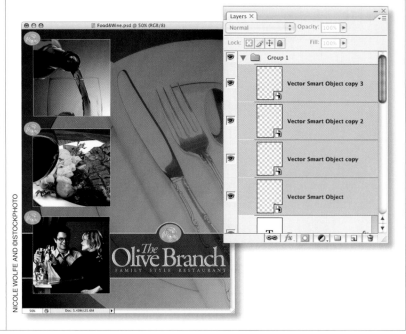

NICOLE WOLFE AND ©ISTOCKPHOTO

With Smart Object layers, all you have to do is double-click on the logo layer in Photoshop. It knows that the artwork originated in Illustrator and will open it in Illustrator automatically. Then you make your changes, save the file, and Photoshop will automatically update each instance of the logo on the Smart Object layers.

DESIGNING TEMPLATES WITH SMART OBJECTS

THE TEMPLATE DESIGNS YOU CAN START BUILDING WITH SMART OBJECT LAYERS ARE AMAZING

Let's face it. The designs you can create with Smart Object layers are not, from a visual aspect, any different from what you could create with regular layers. However, this is one of those tutorials that will blow your mind from an automation standpoint. The way that Smart Object layers can be used to create reusable templates is way cool and truly showcases the power of Smart Objects.

STEP 1: OPEN A PHOTO THAT WILL BE THE MAIN IMAGE FOR AN ALBUM PAGE

Open the main photo for this design. You'll see that the project here works great for creating reusable album pages. These files can be saved and opened later to easily swap out the photo. If you want to try this with the wedding image I used here, you can download it from the website I talked about in the book's introduction.

©ISTOCKPHOTO

STEP 2: TURN THE BACKGROUND LAYER INTO A SMART OBJECT

Start out by turning the Background layer into a Smart Object. In the last tutorial we just used File>Open as Smart Object, but you can turn any layer into a Smart Object, even after it's open. Just Control-click (PC: Right-click) on the layer and choose Convert to Smart Object. Nothing will change visually, but you'll now see the little Smart Object icon on the layer thumbnail in the Layers panel.

STEP 3: DUPLICATE THE SMART OBJECT LAYER

Press Command-J (PC: Ctrl-J) to duplicate the Smart Object layer, so now you have two Smart Object layers.

Select the Rectangular Marquee tool (M) and make a square selection near the top right of the image. Make sure the duplicate copy of the Smart Object layer is the selected layer. Then click on the Add Layer Mask icon at the bottom of the Layers panel to turn the selection into a layer mask.

Now let's resize the Smart Object layer to make it fit into the square area better. Click the Edit menu and choose Free Transform. Press-and-hold the Shift key and drag one of the corner points inward to reduce the size of the photo. Resize it enough so you can still fill the square with the couple kissing. Move your cursor inside the Free Transform bounding box to move it around, then press the Return (PC: Enter) key to commit your transformation.

STEP 6: REPEAT STEPS 3–5 TWO MORE TIMES. PLACE THE DUPLICATES EVENLY ALONG THE RIGHT SIDE

Repeat Steps 3–5 twice. Duplicate the original Smart Object layer, make a selection, add a layer mask, and use Free Transform to reposition each one. Try to vary each photo so it showcases a different part of the photo—almost making it look like there are three different photos, even though they're actually the same one. When you make your selections, arrange them evenly along the right side of the image.

STEP 7: ADD DROP SHADOW, STROKE, AND INNER GLOW LAYER STYLES

Double-click one of the small, square Smart Object layers you just created to open the Layer Style dialog. Add a Drop Shadow layer style and drop the Opacity to 50%. Then add an Inner Glow layer style, changing the color swatch to black and the Blend Mode pop-up menu to Multiply. Finally, add a Stroke layer style. Set the Size to 5 px, Position to Inside, and set the Color to white. Click OK when you're done.

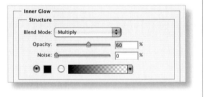

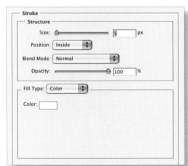

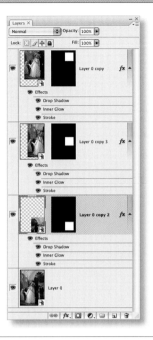

Copy the layer style you just added to the other two square layers. To do this, press-and-hold the Option (PC: Alt) key and click-and-drag the layer style (fx) icon onto the other two layers to duplicate the three layer styles on those layers.

Click once on the bottom layer (the original Smart Object layer). Then click on the Create New Adjustment Layer icon at the bottom of the Layers panel and choose Levels. Drag the black slider under Output Levels to 118 to screen the background photo and make it appear lighter than everything else. Click OK to add the adjustment layer.

STEP 10: APPLY A GAUSSIAN BLUR FILTER ON THE BACKGROUND PHOTO

With the bottom copy of the couple photo still selected, let's add a blur to this layer to enhance its effect as a background design element and not a major player in the whole image. Since the layer is a Smart Object layer, we can take advantage of Smart Filters—you know, the kind you can always come back and change. So, click the Filter menu and choose Blur>Gaussian Blur. Enter a setting of 3 pixels and click OK. Then take a look at the layer in the Layers panel. You'll see the Smart Filters sublayer appear right under it. We don't need to edit it right now, but we will in a moment and you'll see how easy it is.

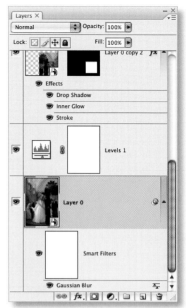

STEP 11: ADD A WHITE RECTANGLE SHAPE LAYER ON THE LEFT

We're just about done. Now select the Rectangle tool (the Shape tool, not the Marquee tool; press U to get it). Press D, then X to set your Foreground color to white. Draw a large rectangle over the left side of the image.

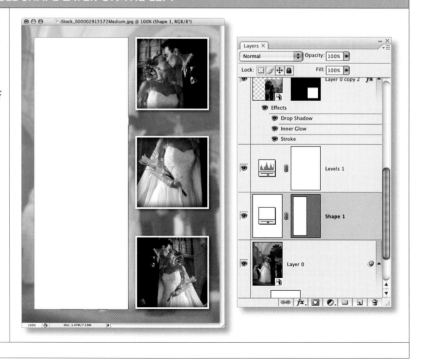

Double-click the Shape layer you just created and add a Stroke layer style. Change the Size to 1 px and the Color to black. Click OK to add the style and close the Layer Style dialog. Then, reduce the Fill of the layer (at the top right of the Layers panel) to 30%. This leaves the Stroke layer style at full opacity, but reduces the white from the layer so you can see through it.

Select the Type tool (T). Click-and-drag inside the white rectangle to create a large text box. Then add some text. I used Edwardian Script for the font and set the font size to 10 pt.

TIP: To increase the space between each line of text, go into the Character panel (Window>Character) and increase the leading amount to 21 pt.

Now for the icing on the cake. What happens when the next project comes along and you have a photo of another couple? Just save this image as a PSD file. Then reopen it when the next project comes along. Click on any of the Smart Object layers, then click the Layer menu and choose Smart Objects>Replace Contents. Find another photo of similar size and orientation and click Place. All four photos are replaced. The size differences are maintained in each of them. The masks stay put. The layer styles carry over and even the Gaussian Blur is applied to the new photo. (You can applaud now.)

The thing that really brings this over the top is that you can move or resize any of the three smaller photos (remember, they're Smart Objects, so you can resize them without losing image quality). So if the new photo doesn't match perfectly, you can change it. Also, look at the Gaussian Blur Smart Filters sublayer. In the new photo it appears too blurry. No problem. Just double-click on Gaussian Blur and adjust the setting. I dropped it down to 2 pixels here and clicked OK. Now that is one heck of a flexible Photoshop document!

LAYERS AND THE CREATIVE SUITE

LAYERS ARE SMART ENOUGH TO BE USEFUL IN OTHER ADOBE CREATIVE SUITE PROGRAMS

Okay, I cheated. This tutorial really isn't all about Smart Object layers. However, it does fall into the "smart" category. It's a quick overview about how smart layers can be with the whole Creative Suite. Plus, I just needed a chapter to put this tutorial into because I think it's important and this seemed like the best option.

STEP 1: OPEN A PSD FILE THAT YOU'D LIKE TO WORK WITH IN OTHER CREATIVE SUITE APPLICATIONS

This really isn't a step. I just wanted to show you that I'm starting out with a PSD file. In this file, I've got Shape layers, Type layers, Smart Objects, and even layer groups. You'll see how these things can be carried over into other Creative Suite applications, such as Illustrator, InDesign, Flash, and Dreamweaver. So, make sure the first thing you do is save your image as a PSD file or none of this will work.

Photoshop and Illustrator probably have the strongest connection of any two programs in the Creative Suite. They really do go together well. For example, open Illustrator. Then choose File>Open. Choose a PSD file and click Open. You'll see the Photoshop Import Options dialog open. Here you can choose to convert your Photoshop layers to objects in Illustrator or flatten them. If you've used layer comps, you can choose one from the list at the top of the dialog. Click OK and your PSD file will open in Illustrator. If you had Type layers, they'll still be editable too.

Now let's take a look at InDesign. When you have a document open in InDesign and you want to put a Photoshop image into it, go to File>Place. Find the PSD file, click Place, and place the Photoshop image just as you would any other graphic in InDesign. Once your image is in, select it and click the Object menu. Choose Object Layer Options. You'll see the layers from your PSD file appear in the Show Layers area of the dialog. Just click the Eye icons next to each layer to show or hide any of those layers in the InDesign file.

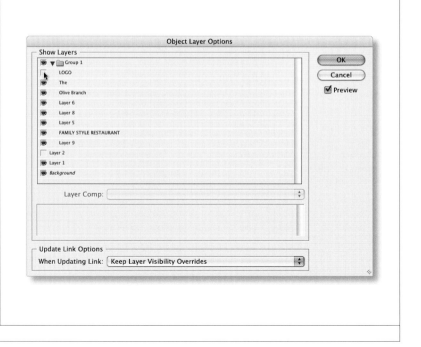

STEP 4: YEP, FLASH LIKES LAYERED PSD FILES, AS WELL

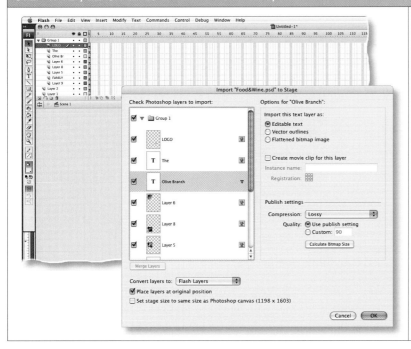

Flash CS3 actually took a huge leap forward when it comes to working with PSD files. To use it, open a project in Flash. Then click the File menu and choose Import>Import to Stage, and a new dialog will open. Here you can see each layer that was in your PSD file, as well as options for how that layer will be handled in Flash. For example, I've clicked on a Type layer here and told Flash to leave it as editable text when it imports it. That way, I'll still be able to change the text later if I need to. Click OK when you're done and you'll see each layer on its own in the timeline.

STEP 5: SAYING LAYERS WORK IN DREAMWEAVER IS A STRETCH, BUT THERE'S A LITTLE INTEGRATION

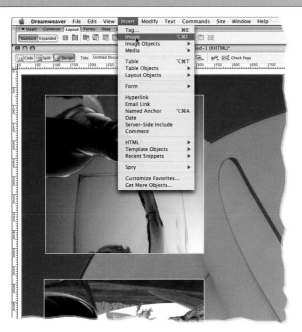

Dreamweaver has some support for PSD files, but not nearly as much as the others. For starters, it doesn't really see the layers in Dreamweaver. You can, however, import a PSD file into a Dreamweaver project by choosing Insert>Image. Then, edit the image by clicking on the Edit button in Dreamweaver's Property Inspector. It'll open the source PSD file in Photoshop with all of the layers still intact. Make any changes that you need, and save the image. Then reinsert the image back into Dreamweaver. Like I said, it ain't much. But hey, it's better than nothing.

HOW DO I LEARN MORE FROM MATT?

SO YOU WANT TO LEARN MORE FROM THE GUY BEHIND THIS BOOK?

You've probably realized that this isn't really a tutorial. However, if you like Matt's lighthearted, yet to-the-point style (like you see here in this book) and you enjoy learning this way, then here are the other things that Matt does.

PHOTOSHOP CS3 KILLER TIPS (WWW.PHOTOSHOPKILLERTIPS.COM)

One of the rules Matt abides by when writing and teaching is this: short and sweet is good. This podcast is a daily podcast, but it only presents one brief killer tip each day. It's short, sweet, and to the point.

PHOTOSHOP USER TV (WWW.PHOTOSHOPUSERTV.COM)

One of the top-rated technology podcasts in the world, *Photoshop User TV* receives millions of downloads each month. Join Matt and his two co-hosts, Scott Kelby and Dave Cross, each week as they share some of the hottest Photoshop tutorials, tips, and tricks. Oh, and they seem to have fun every once in a while, too, so make sure you laugh at the jokes (even if they're bad).

LAYERS MAGAZINE (WWW.LAYERSMAGAZINE.COM)

Matt is also a contributing writer for *Layers* magazine. Here, he gets to flex the Creative Suite portion of his brain, as *Layers* is "the how-to magazine for everything Adobe."

ADOBE PHOTOSHOP LIGHTROOM KILLER TIPS (WWW.LIGHTROOMKILLERTIPS.COM)

Matt also teaches Adobe Photoshop Lightroom. His weekly video podcast and accompanying website follow the same format as Matt's other Photoshop Killer Tips podcast. It's quick and to the point.

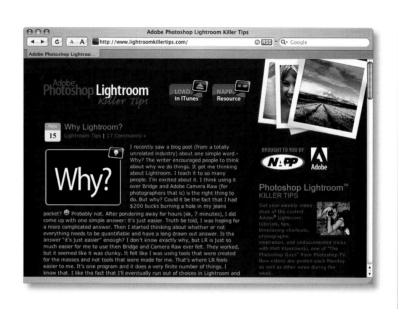

NATIONAL ASSOCIATION OF PHOTOSHOP PROFESSIONALS (WWW.PHOTOSHOPUSER.COM)

This is where Matt works. So if you like his style, then you'll love NAPP. You get a subscription to *Photoshop User* magazine, which is the premier Photoshop magazine, along with online content, forums, tech support, and discounts from a number of retailers.

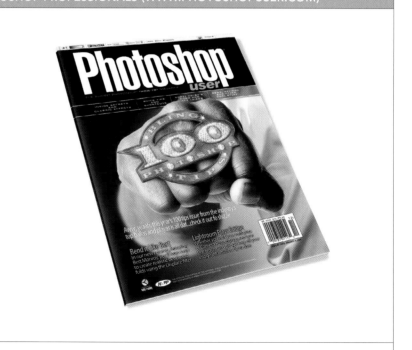

PHOTOSHOP VIDEOS (WWW.KELBYTRAINING.COM)

Matt does DVDs, videos, and online training, too. Again presented in a simple, straightforward, and lighthearted way, you'll find Matt's topics span everything from Photoshop, to Lightroom, all the way to Adobe Illustrator. You can find all of it (plus titles from some other awesome trainers, as well) right here.

PHOTOSHOP WORLD (WWW.PHOTOSHOPWORLD.COM)

Photoshop®
world
CONFERENCE & EXPO

Contrary to what you'd think after reading the other things that Matt does, they actually do let him out of the office from time to time (only twice a year, really). These times happen to be at the Photoshop World Conference & Expo, held once on the East Coast and once on the West Coast each year. Not only will you get live training from Matt, but you can take classes from 30 of his buddies, as well. It's a total Photoshop love fest. You'll love it!

HOW DO I...

? OPEN AN IMAGE AS A SMART OBJECT?

Click the File menu and choose Open as Smart Object. Find the image you want to open and click on the Open button. That image will show up just like normal in the Layers panel, but it will be a Smart Object instead.

? PLACE AN IMAGE INTO AN ALREADY OPEN IMAGE AS A SMART OBJECT?

Click the File menu and choose Place. Navigate to your image and click on the Place button. The placed image will show up as a Smart Object in your image.

? CONVERT A REGULAR LAYER INTO A SMART OBJECT?

You can always go under the Layer menu to Smart Objects>Convert to Smart Object. My favorite way is to Control-click (PC: Right-click) on the layer and choose Convert to Smart Object, instead. It's a lot faster.

? GIVE A LAYER THE ABILITY TO USE SMART FILTERS?

Smart Filters are filters that you can apply to a layer in a nondestructive way. They're a lot like layer styles, so you can always go back and change them. However, Smart Filters will only work on Smart Object layers. If you run a filter on a regular layer, it'll be a permanent change. So convert your layer to a Smart Object before you apply the filter to it. Then, all of the filters you add to that layer will show up as Smart Filters.

? REPLACE A SMART OBJECT?

To replace a smart object on one layer with another image, just click the Layer menu and choose Smart Objects>Replace Smart Object.

? SAVE MY LAYERS SO I CAN USE THEM IN ANOTHER ADOBE CREATIVE SUITE PROGRAM?

All you need to do is make sure you save your file as a Photoshop PSD file. That will give you the greatest compatibility with other Adobe Creative Suite programs. Oh yeah, if the Maximize Compatibility dialog ever pops up when you're saving your images, make sure you always choose to maximize the compatibility. That'll help make sure your images work well with other programs.

Start with an image.

Image created with Adobe Photoshop plus Tiffen Dfx Fog, Cross Process, Day for Night and HFX Grad filters.

Add your creativity.

Dfx™
digital filter suite

- Over 1000 filters and effects for Macintosh and Windows, including Tiffen's optical filters
- 8- or 16-bit/channel processing
- Apply to QuickTime® movies with Photoshop® CS3 Extended
- Standalone application
- Plug-in for still-imaging apps
- Plug-in for video post-production

For a free trial download, go to tiffen.com.

Innovation starts at Tiffen.
The Tiffen Company
90 Oser Avenue
Hauppauge, NY 11788
1.800.645.2522
tiffen.com.

Tiffen and Tiffen Dfx are either registered trademarks or trademarks of The Tiffen Company. All other trademarks are the property of their respective owners.

Get free online access to this book for 45 days!

And get access to thousands more by signing up for a free trial to Safari Books Online!

With the purchase of this book you have instant online, searchable access to it for 45 days on Safari Books Online! And while you're there, be sure to check out Safari Books Online's on-demand digital library and their free trial offer (a separate sign-up process). Safari Books Online subscribers have access to thousands of technical, creative and business books, instructional videos, and articles from the world's leading publishers.

Simply visit www.peachpit.com/safarienabled and enter code UYDKJVH to try it today.